The Art Detective

THE ART DETECTIVE

Fakes, Frauds and Finds
and the Search for Lost Treasures

Philip Mould

VIKING

VIKING
Published by the Penguin Group
Penguin Group (USA) Inc., 375 Hudson Street, New York, New York 10014, U.S.A. • Penguin
Group (Canada), 90 Eglinton Avenue East, Suite 700, Toronto, Ontario, Canada M4P 2Y3 (a division
of Pearson Penguin Canada Inc.) • Penguin Books Ltd, 80 Strand, London WC2R 0RL,
England • Penguin Ireland, 25 St. Stephen's Green, Dublin 2, Ireland (a division of Penguin
Books Ltd) • Penguin Books Australia Ltd, 250 Camberwell Road, Camberwell, Victoria 3124,
Australia (a division of Pearson Australia Group Pty Ltd) • Penguin Books India Pvt Ltd,
11 Community Centre, Panchsheel Park, New Delhi – 110 017, India • Penguin Group (NZ), 67 Apollo
Drive, Rosedale, North Shore 0632, New Zealand (a division of Pearson New Zealand Ltd) • Penguin
Books (South Africa) (Pty) Ltd, 24 Sturdee Avenue, Rosebank, Johannesburg 2196, South Africa

Penguin Books Ltd, Registered Offices:
80 Strand, London WC2R 0RL, England

First American edition
Published in 2010 by Viking Penguin,
a member of Penguin Group (USA) Inc.

10 9 8 7 6 5 4 3 2 1

Published in Great Britain as *Sleuth: The Amazing Quest for Lost Art Treasures* by Harper-
CollinsPublishers.

Grateful acknowledgment is made for permission to reprint an excerpt from "Stopping by Woods on a
Snowy Evening" from *The Poetry of Robert Frost*, edited by Edward Connery Lathem. Copyright 1923,
1969 by Henry Holt and Company. Copyright 1951 by Robert Frost. Reprinted by permission of Henry
Holt and Company, LLC.

LIBRARY OF CONGRESS CATALOGING IN PUBLICATION DATA

Mould, Philip.
[Sleuth]
The art detective : fakes, frauds, and finds and the search for lost treasures / Philip Mould.
p.   cm.
Originally published: Sleuth : the amazing quest for lost art treasures. London :
HarperCollinsPublishers, 2009.
Includes bibliographical references and index.
ISBN 978-0-670-02185-7
1. Art—Expertising—Anecdotes.   I. Title.   II. Title: Fakes, frauds, and finds and the search
for lost treasures.
N8558.M68 2010
702.8'8—dc22   2009049270

Printed in the United States of America
Set in Fournier with OPTI Magna Carta
Designed by Daniel Lagin

*To Oliver, with apologies for the time spent writing
that could have been spent with him*

Contents

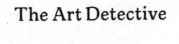

The Art Detective

Introduction

"I suppose you've heard," he began. "In fact it may have been you."

I had no idea what he was talking about. Responding to both my blankness and evident curiosity, he started to play me, alternately giving and taking line.

"It was even on the radio this morning. Surely you must know?" he pressed.

"Know what?"

"About the Rembrandt."

"What Rembrandt?"

"The self-portrait thought to be a later copy or follower. The one with a low estimate of £1,000. Oh, come on, you must have known."

"Sadly not," I replied. "Where was it?"

"Up the road."

Given that the man I was talking to, Mark Ransom, was an

experienced and canny dealer and would award this type of lead-up only to something of great consequence, he now had me hooked. He knew it, and I had no choice but to be hauled to shore at his own pace.

"OK, where up the road?"

"At Moore Allen & Innocent in Cirencester."

He now had me thrashing in the water. I had previewed that actual sale in person two days earlier at the auction house and definitely did not recall anything that could be deemed a great work of art. Certainly not one that approximated to anything by the most famous old master in Western history.

"They say it's the record price paid for a picture at a country auction, apart from anything else," he added with contrived nonchalance.

"What did it make?" I asked weakly.

"With or without auction commission?"

He had toyed with me enough. "Get on with it," I snapped.

After a cruelly protracted pause he mouthed the figure for optimum impact.

"Two—point—six—million—pounds."

The story becomes more stressful. Professor Ernst van de Wetering, one of the greatest art connoisseurs of our times, and specifically of Rembrandt, in the professor's capacity as chairman of the Rembrandt Research Project (RRP), got to hear of its emergence at auction and, unusually for an academic in his position, he issued an invitation to the unknown buyer to show it to him. He later pronounced it a genuine work, not, as it happened, a conventional self-portrait but more a generalized character figure (as distinct from a formal, recognizable portrait), with the new title *Rembrandt Laughing*. As this book goes to print, it has just resurfaced in the art press in relation to a proposed export license (essential for major works of old art leaving the UK) at a valuation rumored to be £20 million.

I still don't know what happened. Damn it, I spent a good half hour wandering around that Cirencester salesroom. I was on holiday, after all, with all the time in the world. Perhaps I did just overlook it—it was a small work on copper—but I also now wonder whether it was being confidentially inspected in a backroom while I was at the preview. Or am I making excuses? I had also failed to flip through the catalogue (a cardinal slipup), where it was illustrated on the front cover no less. All in all, hardly something that as a professional I am proud to own up to, particularly as over the next week I realized just how profoundly I had been out of the loop.

First a restorer told me that he had been sent down to analyze the painting's condition a week before the sale; then a dealer confided that in partnership with another he had been prepared to go up to £500,000; and later I met another who had prepared a bid for twice that amount but did not get his hand up at the sale because the price escalated so fast. The following month I talked with a major London auctioneer who told me that he had been tipped off by one of his clients and had taken the day off to travel down by train to view it. If you add the man who underbid (the distinguished New York dealer Otto Naumann, I later discovered), the successful purchasers who apparently bought on behalf of a private collector and the runners (dealers without galleries who seize opportunities at country sales) who had been aware of it, I can see now that I was naively out of the loop.

This realization in part prompted me to write the present

book. One of the most obvious ways to explain how so many people in different countries were aware of a diminutive painting in a relatively small auction house two and a half hours from London is the technological revolution. The Internet is now an integral tool in the workings of my business. It is amusingly ironic that I, a dealer with a certain knowledge, failed to see something when physically present in an auction room while a shoal of prospective buyers, a large proportion of the informed old-master trade, had been frantically researching and preparing bids for some weeks before the sale after the illustrated catalogue was posted on the auction-house website. Sure, many would have come down to see it as a consequence of what they had seen online, but only as a consequence. And I knew, of course, that it would not just have been the fact that there was a high-quality digital image of the picture for all to find with their search engines, but that with a few clicks of the mouse it could instantly be shared with others: curators, art historians, fellow dealers, prospective clients, all of whom could offer responses, no doubt some of them guarded, which would translate into the type of bidding fervor that was witnessed that day in Cirencester.

This is the culture we now occupy—a market that has a thousand eyes on anything and everything of possible significance that raises its head over the commercial parapet. And it is not just the raw commodity that is so much more accessible, but knowledge too. The ability to research and compare prospective discoveries has developed at the same expansive rate. For the skilled researcher has within immediate reach myriad public collections, archives, articles, price records and biographies that can either shore up or kill a hunch with lightning speed. For a discovery to be established, it has to work on paper as well as in paint. Crucial aspects of a picture's provenance (its history) can sometimes be instantly established, discoveries that fifteen or twenty years ago might have taken days, if not weeks, of professional archival research. In a business fraught with auction deadlines, the Internet's power makes the dealing of the previous generation look like dark prehistory.

Yet it is not just information technology that has progressed, but also technical analysis, the means by which the physical properties of a painting can be diagnosed and understood. Scientists in lab coats are now increasingly entering the formerly forbidden world of artistic attribution. To me one of the most valuable functions of science is to be able to establish a picture's *terminus post quem*, the earliest likely date that it was painted. Databases and other scientific tools still have far to travel in this area, but paint analysis has become more precise in establishing the physical compounds of pigments and the way in which they are applied and, when combined with the use of ever-growing records of when these pigments were first found to have been used and by whom, can add valuable corroborative evidence. Scientific data is one of the bedrocks of the Rembrandt Research Project, the authentication panel chaired by Professor van de Wetering, which I describe in a later chapter. The RRP has helped create convincing arguments that have turned formerly overlooked copies into multimillion-pound originals—and also, sometimes very painfully for the owners, the reverse.

Scientific analysis for the picture hunter has also become much easier to commission. When I first joined the art business, in the mid-1980s, even organizing an X-ray (to ascertain whether an earlier image might be lurking beneath a painting's surface) was a palaver. It meant queuing up on a Monday morning at certain private London hospitals while the less fortunate with damaged limbs waited for the same service. Today a traveling team of professionals in a van not only call round to the restorer or gallery, but also offer other functions, including infrared photography to enable underdrawing—the artist's sketch lines, which can help prove authenticity—to be detected.

Dendrochronology, which dates wood by its tree rings and so provides the probable felling date of the tree from which a painted panel was cut, is now a very precise science, whereas it used to require a lengthy trip out of town for a verdict that later proved to be inaccurate, in many cases because of flaws in the data on which the calculations were made. Not anymore. Men like Professor Peter Klein of the University of Hamburg make regular trips to London, magnifying lens in hand, to offer an on-the-spot service that is both brilliantly precise and of inestimable value to the process of authenticating early works on panel. We now have at our fingertips investigative science that can transform arguments and rule out or bolster speculative claims.

I am constantly told that discoveries are no longer possible with so much airborne knowledge, technology and science; that nothing can remain hidden anymore; that the art world's innocence was last known in the days when auctioneers tipped the contents of stately homes into generalist sales, and if anything was illustrated that was a bonus. In a sense the reverse is true. The world is heaving with paintings that are either unattributed or incorrectly labeled. Certainly there are only a finite number of Rembrandts to uncover, but a discovery is dependent on knowledge that transforms something formerly unrecognized into something that is understood and valued. It also relies on an art market that can then generate buyers. Our culture has new scholarship on all sorts of formerly overlooked artists, and a greater volume of retrievable knowledge than ever before, so opportunities for discovery have greatly multiplied.

The problem, of course, as demonstrated by the Rembrandt, is that the elite hunters of a generation ago have swelled into heaving ranks, and although the potential for discoveries is more abundant, so too are those who can track them down. This does not apply just to dealers but to auctioneers as well, many of whom are considerable authorities in their chosen areas and will take pains to safeguard their reputations and corporate balance sheets. The modern art sleuth has to have not only the advantages of modern technology but something else too. One of the functions of this book is to give the reader a sense of what that might be.

The subject that interests me above all others is the conundrum of condition, and at the end of this book I have included a brief glossary that covers some of the more frequently used restoration terminology. In the case of old pictures, although analytical science or academic knowledge helps, to me the test of a connoisseur is the ability to read what *should* be there but has been obscured or even lost as a result of damage or intervention. It is an uncommon gift but one that characterizes a number of my colleagues, some academics and far from all restorers. Although it is also a product of experience and knowledge, it requires access to imagination and instinct, attributes that are not easily communicable; and as important as recognizing what "cover-ups" and losses actually look like is knowing if, and how, they can be rectified.

Paint on canvas or panel is vulnerable to a hundred different types of onslaught and disfigurement. The most common—and rectifiable—is discolored varnish. An oil painting is normally coated with varnish by the artist to act as a homogenizing "window" through which to view the tones, forms and colors beneath, as well as to provide protection. Varnish also acts over time as a sponge for dirt—anything from tobacco and smoke from a fire to kitchen aromas. Sometimes if these are venomous enough they travel through to the paint layer beneath. A splash of Coke can cause irreparable damage to a painting, but nothing compared with that done to many of the eighteenth-century portraits of the British Raj I recently viewed in Calcutta, which had been so damaged by petrol-engine fumes that the entire underlying paint surface had chemically changed, turning granular. This type of toxic pollution is rare, however, and Coke normally remains in its receptacle until consumed. For the most part tarnishing is benignly confined to the varnish, which can turn as dark as a midnight eclipse: crucially, however, and sometimes more spectacularly than could ever have been forecast, what lies beneath this layer can be recovered.

In a London auction house I once came across a portrait that had been described as a copy of a Gainsborough. The subject was a conventional middle-aged man who was an acquaintance of the artist, and it looked like two centuries of chokingly dirty varnish had never been removed from the painting's surface. It must have been one of those ancestral portraits, lodged uncaringly in some back corridor, its family connections and identity as neglected as its surface, until it turned mahogany brown. Three bright highlights in the hair and one in the collar were all that could be usefully read through the otherwise impenetrable shield of dirt. Speculatively, it looked interesting enough to hazard a bid, and I bought it for £1,200. As it happened, I did so not because I was convinced that a recoverable original lay beneath (although I was hopeful that something of quality lurked in there somewhere) but because I knew that if it turned out not to be I could always sell the frame—high-quality, contemporary and hand carved—and recoup some of my losses.

I hoicked my new acquisition around to my restorer and was then able to witness a graphic process of transformation that has rarely been bettered. In no time at all his worktable top became a mess of filth-saturated cotton swabs as each application dissolved and soaked up more of the two centuries of human, vegetable and mineral accretions that had infiltrated the varnish. It took him less than an hour. One of the dirtiest paintings I have ever bought reappeared like a newborn lamb—a Gainsborough in almost pristine state (a feature of some pictures that remained untouched by early cleaning and restoration processes) gamboled from its confinement. It covered my overheads for three months after I sold it to the American collector Earle Newton.

Even mildly discolored varnish can have a disfiguring effect, particularly for artists whose style relies on glistening, delicate strokes to convey form. In extreme circumstances whites turn syrupy brown, reds go dark brown, blues greenish and blacks turn to pitch. The subtle brush marks that are often found in sky and background and frequently distinguish the work of a master can be entirely lost from view. Assessing pictures in this (superficially) compromised condition requires both an understanding of what cleaning can achieve and faith in what the artist or his school is capable of.

I become frustrated to the point of irate when visiting museum exhibitions where no attempt has been made to explain or interpret the *core* condition of a picture. I am referring here not to pictures that are dirty but to those that have, as happens all too commonly, been *over*cleaned or mutilated. The sensory appreciation of art is governed largely by what remains rather than what the artist first intended, and guidance on how a work might have changed or suffered is as illuminating as focusing on a work that is in a transcendentally good state. Many of the great works of art that constitute the backbone of our visual history do so because of their condition. These are also often the pictures that make the greatest sums at auction, although there is a tendency to attribute this rather numbly to their *quality* rather than more accurately to their notably good *condition*. There are countless thousands of works of art that, had they not been corrupted, would offer a very different picture of our civilization's visual history. Spotting these lame ducks, which in many instances have been demoted by being attributed to lesser artists, and then going some way to reviving them, is another aspect of the quest for lost art treasures.

There barely exists a picture over fifty years old where the paint layer has not suffered, however minutely. The most common malaise is natural degradation. All pigments undergo chemical change over time, particularly when they have been subjected to light. An extreme example is the portraits returned to the great Sir Joshua Reynolds in his own lifetime by clients galled by the disappearance of the flesh tones in their hands, cheeks and jowls as a result of his experiments with pigments. With the passage of years and insensitive cleaning many have gotten worse still. Healthy-looking sitters have taken on the appearance of corpses, ashen white or sometimes gray blue, left with only the bones of his vigorous characterizations and the normally better-preserved clothes to testify to their original impact.

Almost all painters working out a composition will modify first ideas, some slightly, others radically, as part of the natural process of traveling toward the artistic solution. Given that paint often becomes more transparent over time, losing its initial strength of hue, these changes of mind can become visible to subsequent generations. Pentiments, as the results are called, can have the effect of enlivening a composition (they put me in mind of the lines and jottings that cartoonists and draftsmen sometimes put around their figures to express movement) but can occasionally confuse the later eye by introducing distracting shapes and contours. Sometimes restorers are bamboozled, revering the wrong line to the detriment of the artist's intention. One of the National Gallery's most famous pictures, *Noli Me Tangere*, painted by Titian in 1511–12, I believe to be a case in point. Although its authenticity has never been doubted, the picture's powerful emotional tension, achieved by the upward tilt of the recumbent Magdalene's face, is undermined by her uncharacteristically Grecian nose. Carefully examine its outer edge and it is possible to detect the very faint presence of a previous nose, which has been incorporated. It would require no more than a minute glazy stroke to soften it back toward her original Venetian appearance and to heighten the painting's aesthetic and spiritual quality.

Again, this is an area where the risk-taking professional can prosper. In a recent sale in New York there was—to my mind at least—a manifestly authentic portrait of an aging lady by the great seventeenth-century Dutch master Frans Hals. When I examined it first from a digital image it was clear that Hals had originally placed the nose at a different angle, which gave her a mildly Cubist appearance. It had been cautiously catalogued as "Attributed to" the master rather than certainly by him, with an estimate of $300,000–$400,000. All it required was a restorer to knock back the unintended earlier nose to return it to the artist's intended appearance (which we mocked up with Photoshop in the gallery before the sale). Someone else may have come to the same conclusion: the painting tripled the lower estimate to make close to $1 million, and we failed to buy it. The new owner is likely to have something still more valuable if he can persuade the appropriate experts that it is genuine—another aspect of the discovery process, to which I shall return. On many occasions over the past twenty years I have observed how the eye of the academic, dealer and auctioneer alike has been thrown by pentiments, so what is needed is to steer a confident course betwixt reading these marks wrongly and ignoring them.

The most common form of *inflicted* damage to paintings happens by overcleaning—either by chemicals or over-enthusiastic scrubbing—or the process of relining (laying down a perishing old canvas on a new one). The keeper of many pictures in less worldly country houses was often no more than the housekeeper, and the survival of hand-me-down recipes suggests the application of an alphabet of domestic solvents, including urine, lavender, ashes and half-potatoes. Egg whites were sometimes used as an alternative to varnish. More-complicated jobs, such as patching holes, were sometimes given to the estate carpenter. My guess, however, is that these homespun remedies were nowhere near as destructive as those applied by the so-called professional restorers through whose mills passed countless oils in the late nineteenth and early twentieth centuries, a consequence of Europe and America's fast-expanding art market. It hurts me to recall the quantity of pictures I have encountered at auction that have been flayed, crushed and mutilated in order to service the collecting boom during this period. The appeal of a hygienic shiny finish and a swift and cheap process, along with the unexacting standards of an unsophisticated market, gave rise to innumerable acts of destruction. Picture surfaces were pressed so flat under hot irons that much of the paint and the expressive impasto (the thicker, prouder passages of pigment) are now reduced to enameled flatness, their finish reflective enough to shave in. Vicious solvents, ham-fistedly applied, have the destructive power of napalm, and I have witnessed their indiscriminate devastation thousands of times: landscapes stripped of their vegetation, ships of their rigging, faces of eyebrows and figures of feet; delicate afterthoughts, like flying birds, and even signatures chemically dissolved into oblivion.

Although it still happens, restoration has advanced academically, scientifically and culturally, so that the wounding and murder of pictures is less common; but there are very many works that surface at auction and elsewhere that are by major painters but have been demoted because of lack of comprehension about condition. Even if a cataloguer does sense that a painting is attributable to an artist, downgrading it can be a neat means of avoiding having to argue its authenticity, allowing the market to "make up its own mind." Some of the most thrilling discoveries are made as a result of this practice.

As I write these words a vivid example is looking at me

through the open door of my gallery's office, and it lifts my spirits each time I raise my head to meet its glance. The subject is Charles I a few years before his execution. The king's dignified but maudlin appearance was captured at the height of the civil war, during which the English court decamped to Oxford. In highly congested circumstances, and in between battles, the sovereign and his royalists donned armor and silks and sat for their portraits. Even in these siege conditions the court was attended by its portraitist, and after the death of Sir Anthony Van Dyck the mantle had fallen upon an English painter named William Dobson. Only about sixty of his works are known from his short career—he died at the age of thirty-five in 1646—but Dobson combined native empathy with poetic poise. It has been plausibly suggested that he ran short of materials during his two-year confinement in Oxford and so was forced to work on canvases smaller than average and to eke out his paint, a trait that only adds to the realism of his portraits. These are movingly direct, recording the final years of an endangered social order that ended up slaughtered, executed, exiled or dispossessed after its defeat by the parliamentarians. He is one of my favorite painters, in many ways a starting point for a native school of British portraiture that surfaces again with beguiling clarity in the work of Hogarth seventy-five years later.

The portrait was being offered in one of the main London auction houses and we first came across it online, before the catalogue had been printed. I vaguely remembered the picture from when it had been exhibited twelve years before at the Dobson exhibition at the National Portrait Gallery curated by Dr. Malcolm Rogers. But since the emergence of another version of the portrait at Christie's a couple of years later, and the deprecating remarks of the late Sir Oliver Millar, the director of the Royal Collection and the foremost authority on seventeenth-century British painting, the auction house had decided to play it safe and describe it as a copy. From the illustration it even looked that way, and despite the fact that it had a compelling provenance that placed it in the collection of the Dukes of Hamilton, the first of whom enjoyed a close relationship with the king, its flatness and murky tones did little to recommend it. But looking at even good-quality digital images is not the same as physically poring over a work, and this was one I was eager to see again.

We tracked it down in a back corridor of the salesroom, and it took a couple of minutes of fierce flashlight scrutiny to establish what had happened. The painting had been assaulted by ham-fisted restorers. Some seventy-five years or more earlier it had been only partially cleaned and then relined, during which process the remaining fragments of dirty varnish had been crushed into the weave of the original canvas, much as dirt might be stamped into the weave of a rug. These ingrained flecks meant you could not properly read the paint; the modeling was obscured and a noble portrait had taken on the appearance of a place mat. Furthermore a later, now discolored, varnish covered the surface.

Described as "After William Dobson"—in other words a straight copy by another hand—it carried an estimate of £6,000–£8,000. On the basis that the other version by Dobson had made £165,000 at Christie's ten years earlier, combined with the considerable increase in interest in this type of painting over the intervening period, even if it turned out to be a second version by Dobson (rather than the first from-life record) it had the potential to be an important and valuable picture. There was also its lustrous provenance, which we managed to add to.

In this book I explain how the history of a picture can color its appearance. I show how provenance can completely blind eminent authorities into believing a picture is authentic when it is a fake, and also how provenance can unlock a picture's importance and stature. In the case of this painting provenance helped shore up the visual hunch. The portrait was known to have belonged to one of the most eminent families of the seventeenth century, but the earliest certain reference was 1696—close to fifty years after it was likely to have been painted. With a few days to go before the sale, in the inventories of the Duke of Hamilton's pictures, which are archived at the National Portrait Gallery just off Trafalgar Square, we found a reference to the portrait's having hung in the duke's apartment at Holyrood House in 1704, reassuringly listed as the work of William Dobson.

After an auction skirmish we ended up paying rather more than was estimated, at £39,000, but still a great deal less than I had mentally armed myself for. I had it delivered to Simon Gillespie, one of our regular restorers, who had cleaned two Dobsons for me before. Progress through the ingrained dirty varnish using solvents and the tip of a scalpel was understandably slow, but over the course of a morning he was able to expose half the King's face. The contrast with the untreated area was remarkable—one eye and cheek were bathed in silvery light and showed soft, complex modeling. Within a month Simon had managed to unmask the whole image, a convincingly authentic, arresting and formerly hidden face of the executed King of England, now fully accepted as such by Malcolm Rogers.

Art has been deliberately obscured since the earliest times, and for various reasons. Sometimes there were religious or political motives to do so—ninth- and tenth-century Christian murals in the Hagia Sophia in Istanbul, for example, were covered over by the Muslim conquerors in the fifteenth century, just as countless exquisite murals in English and European churches were overpainted during religious purges from the later Middle Ages onward. Sometimes it was done for artistic reasons. From previous centuries there are documented examples of professional artists who, when they were given a fine old master to restore, instead of cleaning and repairing it in the way we understand now, took a brush and repainted it, believing they were simply enhancing the appearance. As I demonstrate in this book, Rembrandt would also employ studio assistants to update his less saleable works, indifferent to the sanctity of his own brushstrokes. On a rather baser level, over the past twenty years I have encountered countless hidden breasts, private parts and double chins, concealed for reasons of prudery or commercial enhancement.

But much the most common purpose of overpaint in the world I occupy is to disguise the scar tissue of damage and restoration: patch-ups, tears, flaking and abrasion and the overly conspicuous cracking known as craquelure. It is the garment of disguise, sometimes cunning, often clumsy, whose function is to trick the eye into believing a surface to be unblemished. Because of the fragile nature of pigments and supports, later paint has been applied to a greater or lesser extent to almost all old paintings, in its most benign and respectable form simply to fill and touch in losses. I defy the reader to find a picture more than a century old in the Metropolitan Museum in New York or the National Gallery in London that has never had any such attention at all, if only at its edges.

Where overpaint becomes contentious and, frankly, compelling to the hunter is when it has been used excessively or in such a way as to disguise the authorship or quality of the work beneath. It is easy to see how it might happen if you place yourself in the boots of a cowboy restorer from a previous generation. You have filled in a hole in the side of, say, a painted horse, but the tone is not perfect. The indentation or bump from the filling or patching also catches the light. Rather than labor to match pigments and perfect the surface, there is a quick fix as practiced by the restorer's equivalent of the builder from hell. By extending the overpaint, spreading and melding it over the horse's flanks, it is possible to largely disguise the handiwork. In so doing, of course, you smother a large tract of the artist's undamaged work. But why give a damn if the client does not notice or care? The painting is still an "original," and it will look superficially smart over the fireplace, particularly if you have cleaned and varnished the whole and left some pivotal areas such as the signature untouched.

Artistic defacing of this type has happened a million times, and the most enthralling instances in my career—those times when the stress and uncertainties of running a business with punishing overheads are justified, when the resolution to live off wits rather than a cozy salary and a guaranteed pension appears not so bad after all, those moments which validate the decision to commit to a world that, however successful, will never get close to the rewards of tycoons I have often supplied— are when these tracts of overpaint are removed to reveal something of artistic value. Archaeologists must sometimes get the same buzz. Although particularly early overpaint can prove either impossible to remove without damaging the underlayer or too costly given the predicted value of the improved picture, in many instances it is viable. The next big question is, why is it there in the first place? Is it applied unnecessarily or in fact there for good reason, covering irreparable damage?

This issue is thoroughly considered in a later chapter, using the example of a major portrait of Elizabeth I, but for me one of the most satisfying and immediate instances in which removal of overpaint caused an ugly duck to mutate into a swan happened a couple of years ago. I was scrolling through eBay in search of portraits. I can't remember what I had entered into the Search field beyond "antique" and "portrait," but amid a gruesome-looking pack of offerings something caught my eye. It was described as American School, nineteenth century, and consisted of a youngish man trussed up in a solid-looking brown jacket. When I clicked on a larger image I was instantly struck by the difference in quality between the head and the body. The features were engaging, well modeled and arresting: the body was boring, inelegant and anatomically uncomfortable. Looking further at the way the paint was applied to the mouth and eyes, I could see it had all the hallmarks of an early Gainsborough. In a later chapter devoted to the discovery of a landscape by the artist, I talk about recognizing the strokes, which is another one of those essential attributes in sleuthing certain types of lost paintings. Given my focus, I have had to get to know the distinguishing style and techniques of a raft of prominent portrait painters. Paint strokes, pigment mixtures and approaches are as varied as fingerprints and similarly incriminating. But why, I asked myself, if the head was by the master, was the torso by what looked like a jobbing sign painter? Was it a hybrid copy? If it was by a copyist, he clearly had not found his true vocation if he could paint a face as well as that. The vendor was a dealer who had no useful information about its history. Further deliberations were hardly necessary, however, as I found myself to be the highest bidder at under $200.

As a (very) amateur naturalist I try to avoid the temptation of using zoomorphic images, as they have a tendency to unsettle people when applied to art, but there is no more apposite way of describing the process that followed than as that of hatching a pupa. When the unframed canvas arrived at my gallery by Federal Express two weeks later I was transfixed by the possibilities of what might emerge; so much so that I shamefully admit to intervening. I took out a bottle of acetone (basically the same as over-the-counter nail polish remover) secreted in my top drawer, together with a bottle of white spirit, and decided to play God. By now I was convinced that the head was by Gainsborough and that there *had* to be a body match. I also have to admit to a certain degree of bravado, owing to the negligible price I had paid for it.

As they say on television, this is not something to do at home without adult supervision—but if I count the months that I have watched it done by consummate experts I have had a long apprenticeship; in fact, I must have witnessed stages in the treatment of thirty or more Gainsboroughs. In idle moments I have thought how enjoyable it would be to be a restorer. Although I lack 90 percent of the necessary patience required, you only have one life, and fantasies provide the ballast. Almost without exception I hand over potential discoveries to the professionals, like delivering a suspect for questioning, so why not live dangerously, I decided, and for once act on my own? I'm unlikely to need to take over the controls of an airplane, or to have to perform an appendectomy on a friend, but this is a world I live and breathe, and my new American suspect presented a consummately exciting opportunity. Deeply aware of the risks, but also confident that I could halt any damage should the operation go wrong, I laid the picture on my block easel and trained the powerful gallery lights on its surface. I put on a pair of magnifying lenses (the same as those used by our restorers), took out my handheld halogen flashlight—invaluable for illuminating details—and placed it within easy reach. I was alone in the gallery and there was nothing to distract me; it was a winter evening, dark outside, and the telephones had stopped ringing.

I began cautiously and haltingly, first applying plain white spirit to the surface of the jacket to see if the paint would react. It was impotent, resting on the surface like rain on a windshield. So I changed to acetone, the restorer's favorite tipple, applying it with a cotton swab to the portrait's right shoulder. I had observed these prudent beginnings a thousand times. Martin Bijl, one of Europe's most celebrated restorers, recounts later in this book the sweaty, physical feeling that engulfs him when he embarks on restoration surgery. Although what I was taking on was child's play in comparison with the technical challenges he confronts, I had something of the same sensation. It gave me a wicked kick. My restorers loathe others touching pictures before they have treated them themselves, and although I pay the bills, they can have a headmasterly way of rebuking me for so much as applying white spirit to a dirty surface—the most benign form of investigation. What, I thought with some amusement, will they have to say when I deliver them a fully autopsied body?

The impact of the acetone was instant. Whatever its makeup, the overpaint had clearly been applied in the past fifty years, and it dissolved like lard. Beneath, I gained through the lenses my first glimpse of the underbody of earlier pigment. I dabbed it with white spirit. Just a few millimeters in diameter, the area was too small for me to assess its quality, but under the halogen light's penetrating beam it looked honest and early. To my relief it also appeared robustly resistant to the solvent.

It may have been the solvent's intoxicating fumes, but my inhibitions began to lift. I realized I had reached the point of no return: it was not the progress of the operation that dictated this, but my own impulses. I found myself incapable of disengaging from the enthralling process of recovering the torso of a dismembered head. What was beginning to appear was clearly of infinitely superior quality, the strokes reminiscent of those in the face. Running throughout the middle of the coat was a series of tears, crudely sealed with white filler, indicating that the canvas had once been ripped. This was the smoking gun I had been looking for, and it now made clear sense: the restorer had succumbed to the easy option and blanketed out his handiwork; but not content with that, he had gone into creative overdrive and redesigned the subject's whole attire.

The floor was now strewn with coagulated brown swabs. An hour had passed and I had developed a steady rhythm—

twizzling the cotton wool onto a stick, dipping it into a cup and rolling it on the picture. With every square centimeter that was revealed, the portrait was cohering into a readable work of art. Areas that at first appeared dislocated mesmerically joined with new ones to form lines and folds. Just as I was reaching the lower-right quadrant, by which time the operation would be complete, I was brought up sharp with a fright. I had hit an area of differently colored pigment. It was pinkish-brown, and for a moment I thought I had uncovered raw ground, the prepared surface of the canvas. Could I have done this or had I encountered the butchery of a previous restorer? I drenched it—and my alarm—in copious white spirit and then angled the picture toward the light. My relief was palpable. Through the spring-clear lens of solution I could read delicate, well-preserved strokes of flesh tone. I had uncovered the edge of a hand, demurely parked into the sitter's waistcoat—one of Gainsborough's neat compositional tricks to conceal anatomy that would otherwise distract.

The following day I sheepishly delivered the stripped-down picture to my restorer Rebecca Gregg, who compliantly agreed to pull it all together. I avoided all conversation about why it exuded the aroma of solvent, had been denuded of its restorations and was covered with the telltale white residue of dried acetone, but I have a strong suspicion she fathomed the reason. Rebecca got to work over the following week. The task involved fastidiously confining restoration to the tears and replicating Gainsborough's glazy finish on top. We ended up with a handsome Ipswich-period Gainsborough that sparkled with jaunty confidence. I do not know who the sitter is; perhaps a local businessman or friend of the artist at the commencement of his adult career. The artist's identity, and that of the subject, had become lost in the annals of time—the fate of many such escapees from Britain, which I touch on in the first chapter. When it later hung in the gallery it was known simply as *Mr. eBay*. Given the zeal of the overpainting, whoever restored it in America must have had no idea he was disguising a Gainsborough.

From my own point of view, having sated my need for risk and adventure in the realm of restoration science and miraculously succeeded in removing the overpaint without damaging the layer beneath, I have no need to repeat the process. My therapy is complete. I also have no other option. Treating me like a drunk, for the past two years my staff have hidden the acetone bottles.

There is an even worse fate that can befall pictures than over-cleaning. They can be chopped up. Sometimes thieves do this to disguise the identity of the stolen goods— it has happened most famously to paintings by Monet and Turner—but it also has been visited on works for commercial or emotional reasons, and I have been involved in a number of instances where, as if by some divine gravitational pull, the disparate halves have rejoined after centuries of separation. If the art of discovery is that of the sleuth, there is no better resolution to a crime than the one we achieved around the time we opened our new gallery on Dover Street, in 2006.

My thirty-year-old researcher, Bendor Grosvenor, whom I shall introduce more fully over the course of the following chapters, was carrying out his daily task of scrolling through the world's offerings. This is a crucial part of his job and one he performs with youthful adeptness, scything through the multi-plicity of available pictures at auction in search of opportuni-ties, combining computer fluency with an incisive eye. He had come across a picture in a New Hampshire auction house and e-mailed it to me to inspect. Described as "Circle of Hogarth," it depicted an engaging young woman in a green dress and mob cap, her attention fixed on a book on her lap, and although half a century earlier, she had the studious introspection of a Jane Austen character. I didn't know who it was by (the digital image was lacking in definition and the painting was evidently dirty), but I judged it to be of sufficient potential quality to be able to attribute it, particularly following cleaning, when such areas as the dress would with luck throw up clues. Drapery can be as illuminating as handwriting in expressing the traits of individ-ual artists.

We bought it for $7,500, and when it arrived a couple of weeks later and we removed it from its crate, it looked more in need of attention than I had bargained for. The color of the dress, which had appeared green, hid another, indeterminable tone beneath, filtered by grimy varnish. Around the body was an accumulation of overpaint covering detail and possibly dam-age too. We decided to suspend judgment until the picture had been restored, again by Rebecca Gregg. A month later, after cleaning and restoration, our lady returned to the gallery a dif-ferent woman. Her complexion had freshened into healthy pinkness and her dress, now freed from the yellow varnish, had become a dramatic, azurite blue, rippling with rococo folds; her left arm now alighted on a table indicated by its elegant, pedestal-footed leg. But it was the *human* leg that had appeared from beneath the overpaint, partly stockinged, thrusting in from the bottom left, that really knocked us back. Midway through restoration Rebecca had telephoned us to announce the beginnings of this shocking emergence, and now it was plain to see. However one looked at it there was no mistaking, and it was too pronounced to be a pentiment. The conclusion was both depressing and intriguing: this limb belonged to a missing figure. Not for the first time, I wearily concluded, we had bought *part* of a larger picture.

Examining the style of the drapery, the confidently described furniture, and the compactly constructed facial structure, I could see enough evidence to state the case for an artist. The one who immediately came to mind was Francis Hayman (1707/8–1776). A leading portrait and subject painter in his day, he had recently made art-world news when the London dealers Agnew's had sold a major example of his work, a group portrait of the novelist Samuel Richardson and his family, to the Tate Gallery for £1 million. Although this painting did not begin to advance toward the stature of that work, he was an artist people rated, with works in many public and private collections, as well as the subject of an exhibition and catalogue by the distinguished art historian Dr. Brian Allen. Bendor immediately got to work minutely comparing Hayman's works with our newfound lady, looking for repeated motifs and comparable stylistic quirks to pin down the attribution. The following day he beckoned me into his office to show me an image on his screen. It was a self-portrait of the artist at the Royal Albert Memorial Museum in Exeter, his city of birth, and it showed him in an artist's cap, palette and brush in hand. He was seated contrapposto, his head facing the viewer but his legs twisting out of the composition. Bendor then flicked up the image of our picture, mounting the two side by side.

Although not known to be half a painting, the emergence of this portrait from America indicated that the Exeter museum's self-portrait had been cut in two. Some periphery canvas was still missing, but that his thigh joined the severed lower leg with seamless logic there could be no doubt: furthermore the easel and canvas in ours now made narrative sense, completing a formalized scene of a man painting himself and his wife in his studio. (Bendor later went down to the museum with our picture and proved it conclusively after a thorough physical inspection of the paint and canvas weave.)

As I looked into the young artist's life, an intriguing hypothesis now offered itself. Hayman married twice. His first marriage, prior to when he was likely to have been painted, ended in divorce, so why should not this be an attempt by him to edit his private history, perhaps on the insistence of his next wife (whom he married in 1752), by removing the offending part? Not enough is known to be conclusive, but clearly something happened to cause what would otherwise be an act of mindless vandalism. We exhibited both halves at our opening exhibition and it caused countless pilgrimages from Exeter and elsewhere to see the reunited couple—a number of visitors questioning the ethics of forcing back together a husband and wife who had chosen to dissociate. Like it or not, however, the young couple are now rejoined for ever, following the Exeter museum's decision to buy the work for its collection.

I write not as a journalist but as a practitioner limited to my own field. For the most part I have chosen examples in which I was directly involved, but there are also cases involving others that I seek to communicate with insights gained from what I do for a living. To the extent that the book deals with fact and not fiction (with the exception of where I slip up, and there are many corners in the art world into which I have barely peered), its scope is curtailed. But then it does not seek to be comprehensive. Its purpose, to use an artistic analogy, is to sketch a number of small scenes and figures by which it is possible to gain a sense of a much bigger composition filled with innumerable paths, dramas, challenges and characters. Although the subject matter is art and the response to art, its discovery and the guile, risk-taking and competition involved in the sleuthing quest are all in the realm of familiar human behavior. The book's other purpose is therefore to highlight the temperaments and motivations of the dealers, art historians, historians, owners and restorers who are drawn to the pursuit of art for reasons of truth, profit or both.

My most lofty ambition here has been to use art as a support for brief character studies, including—in the time-honored Renaissance tradition—a self-portrait or two. Art greatly lends itself to this function. In a secular world in thrall to the cult of genius, as evidenced by the commercial value and sanctity awarded to art by collectors and museums across the world, many deceased artists (and some living) have achieved the status of saints. As Marcel Duchamp put it, for some art is very sedative but not as good as God. Even so, it is tempting to think that art does respond to a crucial need for spiritual sustenance. To own an original Rembrandt (or, in the case of the New York collector Tom Kaplan, eight at the last count) or an authentic Rockwell has something of the allure that holy relics had for the medieval mind. This has spilled over into present-day art dealing, where, when it comes to the work of figures such as Damien Hirst, we have witnessed artifacts being competed for at auction as if they were splinters of the True Cross. Like art itself, the market for its products can be extremely eloquent about human behavior.

CHAPTER 1

The Case of the Hidden Hoard

Far below I began to make out moving lights, uniform blocks and the relentless sprawl of an American city softened by snow. But any sense of relief at coming to the end of a day in the air was short-lived.

For a start, I had no knowledge of the city where I was landing. I also had little notion of where I was off to next. The gentleman I was traveling to meet had told me that the flight would be followed by a two-hour car journey into deep country. Of more concern, however, was the gentleman himself. Apart from that brief meeting in my gallery three months earlier when he appeared unannounced with a suitcase of books and a worn brown envelope of photographs, I had no idea who he was; since then we had only corresponded, and his last letter had contained my plane ticket.

I was now off to spend a weekend with him in the wilderness.

As I write this, close to eighteen years later, I am struck by the quaintness of it all. This was among the last art-dealing forays I was to make in what could be described as the pre-Internet era. I was on my way to survey a collection of paintings that this man had amassed in the 1950s and 1960s. As the photos he had shown me were mostly black-and-white and slightly blurred, it was difficult to assess the works' quality—I needed to see them in the flesh. Who knows, I thought, there may be something exciting there. So I had accepted this stranger's invitation on the basis of a hunch, as well as a taste for adventure, which, as the plane touched down and I faced the realities of my decision, had already begun to pall.

Compare my situation with how we would deal with an "unknown" who walked in from the street today. As soon as he left the gallery, possibly while he was still in it, we would be googling his life and career. It sounds ruthlessly cynical, but in a world full of trickery, duplicity and fantasists, quick access to biographical detail can be invaluable when it comes to apportioning your energies as a gallery owner. Not content with that, I would also ask him to send digital images of the pictures when he returned home—hardly a problem for anybody these days, even with a standard digital camera. If the quality of these proved good enough, from the comfort of my leather chair I would zoom in on the images on-screen, studying them almost as closely as if the paintings themselves were there with me. Only then, once I had gained a strong sense of both the man and his wares, would I consider moving from the gallery.

Instead, as befitted the age, and mine also, I had crashed full tilt into the bleak unknown. The city was Burlington, Vermont, the date November 23, 1992—the day after Thanksgiving—

and the cold air tore into my face as I left the airport and crossed the road to the bus stop where Professor Earle Newton had asked me to meet him. I had forgotten what the old man looked like until I saw again the slightly stooped gait and compressed smile (which I later realized was an almost constant facial feature) as he walked over to greet me. His delivery was frail but measured, his longer sentences ending with noticeable pauses.

"Welcome to Burlington," he said. "You were right on time."

So at least I had met my man. But I did not recognize the looming figure next to him in a duffle coat and jeans. He was heavily built, with black hair, a ruddy complexion and, at odds with the rest of his attire, a tight-fitting chauffeur's cap.

"This is Bill," said Earle.

The big fellow offered me his hand.

"And he's going to drive us," Earle added. "We have quite a journey ahead, so we'd best be off."

Bill picked up one of my pieces of luggage and the three of us made our way toward a formidable but ancient white Daimler parked on the other side of the road, its great chassis spotted with rust. I sat with Earle in the backseat while Bill maneuvered us out of the airport concourse and sedately into the night, heading toward the highway. It was late for me, I felt tired and displaced, and my normal art dealer's patter was not functioning. I kept my gaze fixed, beyond the outline of Bill's large shoulders and peaked cap, on the road ahead. Earle, brushing up next to me in a heavy coat in the darkness, occasionally pointed out sights on the city's skyline as it disappeared from view. By now it had begun to snow.

After we had been traveling for an hour we moved onto smaller roads. There was a distinct absence of traffic and houses, it was deep night, and I became aware that we were driving through a mountain pass, its steep, snow-covered slopes punctuated with irrigation streams.

"Is your home far from here?" I asked as I began to realize that the address I had been given—The Newtons, Route 14, Brookfield, Vermont—was as off the map as it sounded.

"Some way, I'm afraid. The weather isn't helping either," Earle replied.

The wheezing windshield wipers struggled against the splattering snow.

"You see, we don't live in a town or village, so it can be quite a hike when the weather is like this. The nearest grocery store is a half hour."

"That must make shopping a problem," I said as cheerily as I could.

"It certainly does. But there again we are not completely isolated. There are country stores within a couple of miles of our door where you can buy bait and ammunition."

"Oh right," I said, and we reverted to the sound track of the Daimler's rumbling engine and the groan of the wipers.

It was my boyhood friend Charles Glazebrook, who worked with me at my upstairs gallery on Bond Street, who had gotten me to take my first flight to America, two years earlier. He had spent five years working for two leading art-dealing firms in New York before he returned to England, and after a spell as a gallery manager in London, he decided to strike out on his own and to share my premises. He dealt in landscapes, I dealt in portraits, and as we sat at adjacent desks in our brave new venture he would reminisce about his transatlantic experiences—both the good and the bad. As a very young gallery assistant he had lived in a shabby apartment on Manhattan's Upper West Side, so infested with cockroaches that colonies of them scaled his bedroom walls at night. Occasionally, as they traversed the ceiling, he would awake with a start as gravity caused them to plummet down on his face and body. But he also told me of the artistic excitements, the auctions, the dealers and the collectors, and above all of the chance to find and buy British pictures that had escaped our shores in the first half of the twentieth century. I had no choice but to go and find out for myself, he said, or opportunities would elude me.

Buoyed by Charles's anecdotes, I made my initial trip in 1990, when I was twenty-nine. Arriving at JFK, I had only his instructions as to what to do next, which was to take a taxi to my hotel, the Barbizon, and then go to the city's five main auction rooms. My first experience of New York was of two natives of the Big Apple in a tug-of-war with the handles of my suitcase, battling like velociraptors over a fresh kill. Having failed to notice the licensed yellow cab stand, I had fallen foul of the touts. Rattled, I rode with the victor, paying twice the expected fare—my inaugural taste of the land of opportunity.

My specialization then—it has since expanded—was British portraits from Tudor times to the present, and I had given my business the solidly descriptive name of Historical Portraits Ltd. Although portraiture was the height of collecting fashion at the beginning of the twentieth century, the Impressionists and contemporary art replaced them as the trophy aspirations beginning in the 1930s, and American museums, following the trend, had since then been regularly deaccessioning, or selling, old-fashioned British portraits from their holdings, as had private collectors. However, there were still some people who revered interesting portraits, as I did, and to put it crudely these paintings could sometimes be acquired cheaply and sold at a decent margin. So, as a young dealer with very little money, I had the beginnings of an exciting niche. Although to date I had bought only in Britain, where mainstream taste for portraits had similarly waned for all but the best, my business was expanding and I was hungry for new stock.

I established my company on the premise that, with the right research, restoration and marketing, there had to be willing buyers out there, and I had begun two years earlier by offering to the sitters' descendants antique portraits that I had been able to pick up in minor London and country sales. Trade had since grown to include portraits of famous British figures—kings, queens, poets, politicians and writers—as well as works by the more major painters, whose styles I had begun to recognize. The most exhilarating opportunities were when I was able to buy sleepers at auction, miscatalogued lots where the artist or sitter had been entirely missed, and there was the potential to re-offer them at another auction, or sell them privately, for a substantial profit.

On my first trip to America I met three people who have remained close friends and trade allies to this day. Peggy Stone from Doyle auctioneers was the first. She was in her last few months in the job, having recently decided to join her husband, Larry Steigrad, who that month began to go it alone after working for ten years with Bob Haboldt, a leading old-master dealer in Manhattan. Peggy was intrigued when I asked her to show me all the unsold portraits from the auction house's racks—paintings that had failed to sell at previous auctions—and I ended up buying two in private deals from the unsuccessful vendors the following day.

Peggy wasted no time telephoning her close friend Rachel Kaminsky, who worked at Christie's, to tell her, "We've got a live one here. He wants all our unsold faces," and my next meeting was with Rachel in her auction room's storeroom, where I succeeded in buying two more BIs ("bought-ins," or unsold lots). Peggy next told her husband about this mug from London and he invited me over to their apartment. After protracted haggling Larry sold me his first picture as a sole trader: a William Wissing of two children in a landscape. (Gallingly, five years later he told me I could have gotten it for $2,000 less had I not buckled first in the negotiations.) Having acquired more pictures in the main public auctions on Thursday and Friday, at the end of that week I checked in at the airport with twelve hand-carried British portraits, and my love affair with America began.

I also realized that I had competition, although the immediate outcome was that it paid for my trip while I was still in the States. I had managed to buy for $2,000 in Christie's East (the then lesser arm of the main auction house) a seventeenth-century French portrait described as being of an unknown man but whom I recognized as Louis XIV. Even though my focus was British, there must be someone in London, I surmised, who would want a portrait of France's Sun King. In my hotel room the following day I received a message via Christie's to telephone a Mr. Jenkins. I assumed it was the wrong number when it was answered by a man who announced himself as "the sacristan." He then pointed out it was *Father* Jenkins I wanted, but that he was currently taking confession. An hour later he telephoned.

"I believe you were the buyer of the unknown Frenchman." The voice was New York Irish.

"You mean Louis XIV," I replied.

"OK, so you got there too. Would you take a quick profit? I had left a low bid and was hoping to buy it cheaply. I collect paintings, and he's a subject I admire."

I sold it to him for $3,500, and so not only sold my first American sleeper, but made my first American client—and a priest into the bargain.

In those days there was no choice but to go out and see the auctions, dealers and private collections, and while I still make regular trips to the States, so much more evaluation and buying can now be done remotely via digital images. Early in my career, catalogue images, particularly when it came to portraits, were often little more than stamp size and furthermore, my experience at reading authorship and condition from an illustration was nowhere near as honed as it is today, given the deeply instructive experience of both failure and success. Our scope has dramatically increased too. Bendor Grosvenor, my researcher, a child of the technical revolution, can sift through hundreds of such items a day. His search engines corral offerings with luxurious ease from across America and the rest of the world, and we now buy up to three pictures a week without seeing them in person.

In 1992, with limited staff and less technology than now, there was little option but to travel, and I found myself going to New York three times a year. Earle Newton, a bolt from the unknown, had found me after a recommendation from another dealer, who, knowing of my specialization, had simply passed him on. Hence another voyage across the pond, to meet the man. This time it was into entirely uncharted territory.

The Daimler made its steady way down from the pass

through a long, flat valley laced with fast streams. I was increasingly weary, and given the antiquity of the car's heating system, by now rather cold as well. Looking at my watch and realizing that I was still on British time, I set the hands back to early evening. We had been on the road for two and a half hours and I was about to ask Earle how much farther it was, when I felt the engine slow down.

"Home at last," he said. The headlights shone along a snowy driveway and onto a large, white-painted clapboard house with green shutters, the Stars and Stripes fluttering from the front porch. The porch door was already opening as I clambered out of the well-like leather seats, to be greeted by a fine-boned lady in her seventies, the orange light of the house's interior shining through her permed blonde hair and outlining her slim body.

"Welcome to Vermont," she said, offering me her hand. "I'm Jo, Earle's wife. Come on in. We've been waiting for you."

She ushered me into a large, low-ceilinged family room and as my eyes became accustomed to the light I noticed at the far end a table formally laid for a Thanksgiving dinner with elegant glasses, tureens and blue china plates. The house was book-filled and warmly embalmed against the elements by its wooden walls. As I sat in an armchair with a cup of tea I felt tranquilized by the heat of the room and by fatigue as twelve hours of travel and the five-hour time difference took full effect. Yet I still had enough wits in play to look around and, despite the relief of having arrived at my destination to such a pleasant welcome, I began to be aware that something was not quite right. My unease took a few minutes to form and then grew rapidly into a sickly sense of apprehension.

Every successful art dealer I know has mastered the reflex of surfing the pictures on entering a room. There is nothing particularly predatory in this, just professional survivalism, and as I had crossed the Atlantic to see a substantial art collection I was naturally expecting to encounter evidence from the outset. But, although the walls were decorated with ornamental prints and framed photographs, and the shelves with numerous ornaments and knickknacks, there was not an oil painting, or even a frame, in sight. Had I been asked to guess the owners' professions from the interior of their home, apart from noting that they had an interest in reading, as there were magazines, paperbacks and large hardback books everywhere, I would have hesitated to describe them as anything more than a modest middle-class family, perhaps schoolteachers. Globetrotting art collectors they were not.

I tried to recall what Earle had shown me in that envelope in my gallery. They were definitely oil paintings, originals I remember him telling me. And I recollected studying the images and, despite their blurriness, thinking that they looked like genuine works replete with blemishes and original frames. After all, it was what I did regularly as a dealer in those days, reading through endless catalogues, assessing and judging potential opportunities from rudimentary photographs. Yet it now appeared that there was nothing that would even have passed for an original in the main downstairs room. What, I asked myself, if there were no paintings at all? What if they were no more than photographs or he had borrowed them from elsewhere? Had I just crossed the Atlantic and been drawn into the home of a (with any luck) well-meaning lunatic?

Earle showed me upstairs and along a narrow corridor to my room (again, no paintings) but suggested I come back down shortly for dinner, which, he stated with a touch of ceremony, had been delayed in honor of my arrival. In due course I took my seat at the table and was wondering, in my agitated and exhausted state, how I could rally the appetite to eat, let alone speak at this late hour, when I noticed the extra setting.

"Are we expecting somebody else?" I asked.

"Only our son, Bill," replied Mrs. Newton. A minute or two later the front door opened with a gale of cold air and the chauffeur, minus his hat, took his seat at the end of the table. I suppressed my surprise and noticed him exchange smiles with his mother, which he continued to do throughout the evening. Clearly I had missed something at the introduction stage earlier, I tried to reassure myself. Earle took the seat opposite me and his wife brought in from the kitchen a large turkey and a bowl of sweet potatoes. Clasping her hands in prayer, Mrs. Newton then addressed both God and ourselves with words I can clearly recall:

"Dear Lord, thank you for sending Philip to us. Over the next two days we hope there will be surprises and excitements for us all. May he not be disappointed, and may we learn from him."

My amen could be heard above the others.

I can't remember much of the dinner that night, apart from my first taste of sweet potato, but with Mrs. Newton's encouragement I disclosed something of my home life in London as a bachelor, and spoke about my parents and siblings, a subject that seemed to animate her. As well as Bill, she told me, they had a daughter who worked in corporate business in New York. She herself had retired as a primary-school teacher ten years earlier but now had an active part in the local church, where she played the organ. Her chatter was affirmatively maternal, and I began to find myself reflecting that if this were some sort of setup, she surely could not be any part of it—or must at least be oblivious to it.

Nothing was said of the Newtons' own collecting, however, and when I found a natural moment in the conversation to ask where his pictures were, Earle merely responded by saying that all would be revealed in the morning. All the while I could not help observing Bill at the end of the table, who had cut up the turkey with dexterous strokes but remained largely silent. I fathomed that he lived in one of the upstairs guest rooms and had recently settled at home after finishing a job running, bizarrely, a milking dairy in Riyadh. He now helped his father and mother and made furniture as a hobby. A big-framed man I guessed to be in his midforties, he presented a curious figure in the family dynamic. I could detect, despite his kindly, rubicund cheeks, an air of preoccupation.

All the while Earle's fixed smile rarely left his face, and realizing that my conversation was slowing, he suggested that I take myself off to bed. He anticipated, he told me, a full day of activity starting early in the morning.

I fell asleep immediately but woke with a start around 4 A.M., and it took me a full ten seconds to work out where I was and then to ask the question: What the hell have I gotten myself into? Peering out the window, I could see barely anything except snow and darkness and the looming white shape of another building across the road. I also badly needed to go to the loo. The house was entirely silent except for the slight groan of floorboards as I made my way out of the small bedroom to where I recalled the bathroom was located. Groggily I pushed the door, felt for the light switch, and found that I had walked into an unused bedroom: unused, that is, for sleeping. I stood in front of an impregnable fortress of books, stacked in piles five feet high and covering the whole floor. I had never seen so many concentrated in such a small space, and accompanying this tonnage of aging tomes was a sweet odor of decaying paper, which somehow seemed all the more pungent when I noticed an ominous water stain on the ceiling. Quietly closing the door, I found the bathroom and then returned to bed.

After dozing considerably longer than I had intended, I came downstairs for breakfast to find the day had already begun for the family. Earle was standing there in a light-blue tweed jacket, a large key in his hand.

"I want you first to meet India, my sister, who lives across the road," he beamed. "She's a most interesting woman and has a large collection of books. I know she will enjoy seeing you."

What is it with this family and books? I pondered as a short while later we crunched out into the snow to meet India. The sun was shining and the glistening morning light began to revive my spirits, not least because I could see we were not as secluded as I thought. Across the road was a white clapboard church, its paintwork somewhat neglected, with a sign on a pole that read "Museum of the Americas." A little farther down, in the direction in which we were walking, was a trailer with a large, somewhat makeshift extension attached to its rear.

"Are these yours?" I asked as we passed a large barn and garage on the other side of the road. But it was what was parked around the building that I was referring to. There, in varying states of rust and rot, stood twenty or more cars, mostly long-chassis period pieces from the fifties and sixties, including Chryslers and Lincolns like those reconditioned numbers still being driven around Cuba today. There was even a London black cab. Mostly with deflated tires, they looked like decaying carcasses, and nature was fast taking over; one even had a tree growing up through it.

"Yes," Earle replied. "I collect them. There'll come a day when they are appreciated, but there's nowhere else to store them."

He rapped on the door of the trailer-house and we were beckoned in by a lady in her seventies seated in an armchair. India had pronounced, linear features and her eyes suggested the same penetrating intelligence as her brother's. Around her neck was a heavy necklace of semiprecious stones, harmoniously matching the rest of the grotto-like dwelling, which brimmed with Oriental vases, figurines and ornaments. Behind, deeper into the recesses of her strange home, was a library of scrupulously ordered books, to which she guided my eye. She did so with pride, gesturing toward rare and important items among them.

"I'm going to make sure Earle doesn't get his hands on these, else they'll decompose like the rest of them," she blurted with unexpected fierceness. I turned to her face in search of irony or humor but, apart from a token softening of the extremities of her mouth, saw none.

Earle absorbed the slur, if anything appearing rather proud of his outspoken sister. After asking about her interest in collecting, I gathered she had obtained a degree in librarianship—hence the books—and had spent time in the Far East, where, as part of a U.S. government program, she entertained and edified

American servicemen. It was there she had started collecting Oriental antiques.

"I never married, though," she said emphatically, "because I have never seen a man as smart as I am."

Earle had clearly been keen to demonstrate the impressive bluestocking intelligence and connoisseurship of this blood relation; whereas he had been content to have his son drive us in near-silence for well over two hours. Our visit concluded, he promptly led me out of the trailer toward the church with the promise of something of his to see.

The key to the main door did not open at first and Earle had to go and get help from Bill, who then quickley returned to the house. Earle shuffled around to find the switches, discoursing from the cavernous interior.

"We call this the Museum of the Americas," he began with pride and a touch of formality, as if this were a practiced opening line. "Our aim is to tell the story of America and how it grew out of its relationship with Britain. Everything from our culture to our legal system evolved from there."

"Do you get many visitors?" I asked.

"About three or four a month on the weekends. That's when we're open," he replied from the darkness.

If this was all a great hoax, I reflected, at least it now seemed I had arrived at the denouement. As I stood in the doorway of the church my eyes gradually became accustomed to the low light inside and I began to notice that there were chairs for the faithful—except that, propped against them and on the seats, instead of people, there were square and rectangular shapes.

When Earle turned on the overhead lights I was presented with a sight that all these years later is still as fresh in my mind as yesterday. There was indeed a congregation: not of people but of seventeenth- and eighteenth-century portraits, close to three hundred in total, not only on the chairs but covering or filling every available hanging space, niche and corner. I walked slowly down the aisle. Works by Reynolds, Lely and Soest hung where the Stations of the Cross once were—it had been a Catholic church—and many others by lesser artists were propped against the perimeter wall, some in stacks. The chancel was double-hung with works by American painters such as Gilbert Stuart and Robert Feke. Everywhere I looked, faces of antiquity, some framed, others just canvases, blinked back as if surprised by the sudden flood of light.

This was not a museum collection, it was a hidden hoard; not least because the way the pictures were stored and hung, many without labels, gave it the look of a glorious stately house sale in which the untouched contents of the attic had been temporarily tipped into the reception rooms on view day. The condition of the paintings added to this impression. Like the cars, many were in various states of decay. Mildew covered the surfaces of a pair of portraits, of a seventeenth-century nobleman and his wife, which leaned against the wall: a whitish cloud ran from the top edge of each canvas and, like a lace veil, completely covered the features of the man save for his nose, which remained oddly untouched by the fungus. Canvases hung loosely on their stretchers like flapping sails, the prolonged effects of damp, neglect and lack of keys (the wooden pegs that keep a canvas tight) rendering the image unreadable unless angled toward the overhead track lights. Others had not been cleaned for a century or more, their fresh Anglo-Saxon flesh tones fusing with the discolored varnish to produce an ethnic hue which artist and sitters alike would have been taken aback to behold.

"Most of these I bought in the late fifties and sixties, when you could pick them up cheaply," Earle explained. "Sometimes I'd purchase them at auction, sight unseen, and on one occasion I managed to buy a stack of five for $100 from a dealer who had bought them for their frames. You see, I'm not a wealthy man. I just did what I could with the means available."

Propped against the altar, one picture in particular now lured me. It stood out partly because of its quality but also because it did not conform to the politer, better-behaved expressions all around it. An unashamedly porcine image of a middle-aged woman in pink taffeta, she had the unfashionable hint of a smile showing through her bulbous cheeks. Its candor was mesmeric.

"Who is she?" I asked. As I did so I knew that there was only one artist capable of pulling off this feat of originality. A savage satirist of society, he could not rid himself of the very thing that made him so great: a compellingly honest response to his sitters. I had never seen this picture before, and finding it in a deserted church in Vermont was reason alone for the journey.

"I'm glad you spotted that," said Earle. "That was my most expensive portrait from the early days—it cost me $250. They told me it was by Hogarth. Do you think otherwise?"

"Not at all," I replied. "It's astonishing." I was looking at a picture worth between $400,000 and $600,000.

For the rest of the days we went through the portraits one by one—me with my flashlight assessing them, he writing on his notepad. Earle had bought a large proportion of the paintings for their appearance, without secure knowledge of the artist, and given that this was what I did for a living I had the thrill of christening many of them with attributions. Although there were some very substandard works, as you would expect from his shrimp-net style of buying, there were also others, by artists such as Joseph Wright of Derby, George Romney, Jonathan Richardson and Sir Godfrey Kneller, that were entirely authentic, and I had the captivating sensation of taking the lid off a cache of lost heritage, an undisturbed burial site of English and American portraits. As he had been buying mostly in the 1950s and '60s, when British art was in the extreme doldrums commercially and middle-ranking British portraits could be bought very inexpensively, he had been able to amass a collection of notable diversity and quality. Unless they were by major names like Van Dyck or Gainsborough or Copley—in which case there were people like Paul Mellon coming to the fore who were keen to add them to their more loftily ambitious collections—more obscure portraits, particularly if not obviously decorative, would struggle to find buyers, and at that time there was little incentive or expertise to catalogue them accurately. On frequent trips around America and to London and Europe, Earle had applied the same rationale to this genre of art as he had to other commodities, such as cars, books and, as it later emerged, broken-down houses as well: if something was giveaway cheap—and that was an abiding qualification—and had some connection to history, art, design or literature, he hoovered it up. On one occasion he noticed a beaten-up period car on the main street of the village and contacted the owner to ask whether he was interested in selling. "Happily," he replied. "Except you already bought it from me a few months ago."

What appeared to elevate his purpose above that of the pathological hoarder was a greater ambition, to which he constantly referred throughout our cataloguing: the desire to bequeath his objects and collections to a teaching institution to help champion the history of his nation and, in particular, its relationship to Britain.

Over dinner that night I learned more. Bill was absent, but Jo, retaining a lamplike family pride and affection at the end of the table, began by telling me how she had met Earle in high school and they were married at the university chapel upon graduation. The man she was hitched to did not keep still: over the next half century they would live in thirty different locations in pursuit of his career and interests. He, in turn, opened up about his desire to collect, acknowledging that there was a crucial distinction between himself and his wife.

"I collect things, and Jo collects people." He grinned, enjoying the pithy clarity of his summation.

Earle's love of objects and craft surfaced when he was unusually young, and in an intriguing way. At thirteen he set up his own printing press at his parents' home. Although it remained small-scale, mostly for cards, pamphlets and letterheads, he continued to operate it during summer vacations while he was studying at Amherst College, in Massachusetts, where he came to the notice of the celebrated American poet Robert Frost, who granted him the first opportunity to print his poem "The Gold Hesperidee"—a great accolade for the earnest young student. Earle's mother, an accomplished artist, illustrated the cover. In time not only did he become a professor of history at Norwich University in Vermont, but over the next fifty years he held an extraordinary range of cultural posts, including ten directorships of preservation, historical, and archival bodies and societies. Teaching history, Earle told me, had always been his calling, and he had been a Fulbright Scholar in the 1950s and attached to both Bristol and London universities in England, where he also picked up a diploma in museum administration.

It had struck me as rather amazing that a man with relatively little money had been able to acquire so much, particularly when I learned that he had managed to buy sixteen houses in America and England as well. His life was a constant mission, and in the past ten years he had been away from home for up to six months a year, his eye forever on property and collecting opportunities. He would find termite-ridden houses in run-down areas that no one would dare touch and slowly refurbish them. He lived frugally, abhorred spending money on anything he could avoid, and by occasionally selling and always conservatively investing the proceeds (I later heard he had nineteen bank accounts and twenty-five little funds) he had managed to create the means to indulge his desire to collect. Partly because of his thrift, when it came to paintings and art objects he confined himself to buying things that others for the most part disregarded but which, in his view, would one day be of historical value. By seeking to predict future value rather than respond to present fashions, he was able, despite a limited budget, to pursue a wide-ranging buying policy. As I also discovered that night, he was aided in this by a pronounced intellect. Although his delivery was slow and occasionally aged-sounding, Earle had a deep knowledge of many subjects, both contemporary and historical, with a quiver of formulated views on any moral issues involved. Above all, he deemed history and its study vital for addressing the problems of the present day, and his collecting was an extension of this.

I spent the next day documenting the collection, and every so often Bill would be summoned to photograph a picture or its reverse if it seemed to hold further clues about the artist or the sitter for future research. Bill and I had occasional conversations and he led me to the basement to see an impressive piece of craftsmanship, a cabinet that he had designed and made himself. But it was clear from what he said that he did not have a great interest in his father's collecting eccentricities, and he explained that he simply needed to be around to look after the museum, his mother and his aunt when his father was away. This, it became apparent, was now his life.

I had arranged to take a bus to the airport the following morning, and before he dropped me off at the bus station, Earle addressed the subject of my fee for cataloguing the collection—a task that was far from complete but which I had started by making thirty or so new attributions and confirming or de-attributing many of the other works.

"I would rather not give you money, but instead would like you to take something," he said, with what I was now recognizing as characteristic frugality.

That suited me, and I began to consider the possibilities. I would happily have taken the Hogarth but somehow felt that he did not have that in mind. Instead he led me toward the garage, and when we had negotiated our way through the defunct luxury motors he heaved open one of the wooden doors. Inside were more vehicles, but they were largely obscured by the incalculable quantity of objects that filled every shelf or were heaped in piles or falling out of overfilled boxes on the floor. At least, I thought, he is not intending to give me a car, but the more I considered the options the less thrilled I became. That same boundless ardor that he had directed toward acquiring his portraits he had also let loose on lesser things. Stuffed animals, dolls, pots and pans, typewriters, giant old commercial photocopiers and large cabinet TVs filled the foreground, while bathtubs, lavatories and showerheads provided the backdrop (these I later gathered were for his houses).

Peering into the box nearest to me I saw unopened pocket calculators, plastic talking parrots and toy cars.

"This is what I thought you might like," Earle said, dislodging from within the confusion between two old radios a small painting. It was an oil sketch of the River Stour in Suffolk, with a streak of crimson sky and flecks of white paint to suggest cattle. "I bought it for £12 in an antique shop in Windsor in the seventies. They said it had a chance of being by John Constable, but since I don't collect landscapes, would you like to take this?"

I scrutinized the strokes and noticed a chilled varnish, partly caused by damp, muting the tones. There were also crease marks running through the canvas, suggesting that at some time in its early life it had been folded to fit in a box or an envelope. It had potential and, looking at the rest of the possible items around me, I spent little time in deliberation.

"Done," I said.

I felt a little nostalgic as I said goodbye. Jo stood on the porch and made me promise to return, saying she wanted me to meet her daughter too. I then called by the trailer to see India, who expressed similar sentiments and made another joke about the decrepitude of her brother's storage arrangements. Bill emerged from the house, this time without his chauffeur's cap, and once again I clambered into the old Daimler with him and Earle. This strange community with its hidden secrets had rather bewitched me. Later, as he saw me off, Earle said, "I see all this as an undertaking, and I will continue to come to London. Please be sure to come back too, as there's still a lot to do."

I did return, over two years later, but in the meantime back on Bond Street we continued to catalogue the collection from photographs in the National Portrait Gallery's archives, the Witt Library at the Courtauld Gallery and other repositories of art history indispensable to the rescue of lost information on artists' identities and works. The little landscape turned out to be a genuine Constable, an unknown plein air (outdoor) sketch of the river Stour next to Dedham, the village where he lived and worked. I sold it to an American collector and it amply covered the time we needed to allocate to the project of bringing Earle's collection to life—something which, to my pleasure, I was later to discover bore fruit for his greater purpose. Earle visited me at least three more times at my first-floor gallery on Bond Street, and I noticed that he was slower and more infirm on each trip. On his last visit I witnessed him crying. Bill, he told me, was suffering from advanced osteoporosis that was further complicated by liver disease, and although he was receiving the best medical help it seemed he had lost the will to live. Six months later he was dead.

But Earle's age and grief did not impede his indomitable will, and he had even managed to buy another house in England, at Horncastle in Lincolnshire, where he stayed in shabby circumstances for weeks at a time and made day trips around England by bus and train. We even swapped a few pictures. His collection lacked a Gainsborough, and I exchanged one for a work by Jonathan Richardson, a fascinating portrait of his virtuosic artist son, likewise named Jonathan Richardson, with his pictures and sculptures around him. It hangs in my house to this day.

We rather lost touch in the last few years of Earle's life, but in 2006 I received an e-mail from his daughter, Toni, whom I had still not met, saying that he had died in Florida at his home after six months in a nursing home. I sent my condolences and in reply Toni suggested I visit her and her mother in Florida, where they now lived, to see what had happened to the collection. Totally unknown to me, Earle had given it all to the Savannah College of Art and Design, in Georgia, together with his books and prints, and now there is a building dedicated to him. So in 2008 I flew to Jacksonville, from where Toni and her (relatively recently acquired) husband, Clark Townsend, drove me to the college, where I was able to witness for myself how the shambolic contents of a defunct church had mutated into a part of the national heritage.

It was difficult to comprehend how radically the collection had been elevated. I inhaled deeply as we drew up before the magnificent nineteenth-century Doric-colonnaded Greek Revival building on Savannah's Martin Luther King Jr. Boulevard. Beneath the pedimented façade was a smart circular sign that announced: "The Earle W. Newton Center for British and American Studies." Inside, capacious rooms with polished pine floors created the atmosphere of a historical pantheon and, instead of hanging by nails from a tongue-and-groove wall or being stacked haphazardly in piles, the better portraits were mounted loftily beneath elaborate stucco ceilings in a scientifically controlled, museum-compliant environment; they were also labeled, carefully framed, and lit with institutional reverence. Gratifyingly, given their previous state, many of the paintings had been rejuvenated, returned to their former colors and contours by restorers from across America. The college— it claims to be the largest in America for art—had been overjoyed to receive the collection, which, together with Earle's accompanying endowments, had been valued at nearly $9 million. At the inauguration ceremony in 2002, attended by the British consul general as proxy to the Queen, Earle and his family received a standing ovation, and the college's president, Paula Wallace, was suitably humbled by the donor's generosity. She talked of how the collection would give students an opportunity to study works first hand, which "will enhance academic studies . . . inspiring new research and creative endeavors" and how the center had been drawing twelve thousand visitors a year. Earle was also made an OBE (officer of the Order of the British Empire) by Buckingham Palace for his cultural contribution to the history of Britain.

During the car journey to Savannah I had the opportunity to ask Toni some questions. Her husband drove, she next to him, me sitting in the backseat taking notes, trying to get a sense of how it all had worked. Although I knew Earle had a small amount of money as well as an academic's salary, it was still a mystery how he had accumulated such a bequest and, as it now turned out, had also left ample for his wife, who lived in a luxurious Floridian suburb. I wanted too to know what happened to the rest of his possessions. Toni rolled her powerful blue eyes when I recalled the cars. At the age of sixty she was a strikingly good-looking woman with a tall, statuesque figure, her mother's thick hair (in her case brunette) and vivid strokes of red lipstick that accented her upfront manner. Her recollections of her father were an uncomfortable revelation: a combination of genuine affection and unsettling honesty.

At Earle's death, she told me, the automobiles at his various houses had numbered some sixty in all. Some had become half buried under rotting leaves and the branches of trees others had become infested with rodents, and for the most part they had rusted into the ground. In Vermont the leaking oil from disintegrating engines had begun to pollute the waterway, much to the consternation of local officials. Many of the books had not made it through the intervening decade either. Snow had collected in the roof of the family house, turned to ice, and when it melted burst through the ceiling of the book-filled bedroom I had stumbled on that first night in Vermont, reducing most of them to pulp. When I asked about the houses, the story was similarly grim. Earle had rarely if ever finished a project before he was on to the next, and many of them stood around in dour states of decay or unresolved restoration, their roofs leaking and timbers collapsed.

"He was an amazing man, my dad," said Toni. "What he achieved was outstanding. I was captivated by everything he managed to attain. But he had his eccentricities." The more I heard about these foibles, the greater the price, I realized, not he but his family had had to pay for the great cultural legacy to Savannah.

Earle was so blighted by parsimony that on occasion he had left the family almost destitute. Although I had gathered he was a man who abhorred overspending, I had not appreciated the extent of his aversion. Toni began by telling me about the little things—how he would always try to pay at pharmacies or restaurants with coupons, which he avidly collected, presenting them even if they were out-of-date and scratching his head to feign ignorance when challenged. He rarely if ever tipped, once returning to the table to remove money that another family member had left. At buffets he would trouser food and Jo would find pieces of pie and cookies in his pockets. What was more serious, however, was that he would avoid paying bills whenever he could get away with it, absenting himself not just when it came to settling up for a meal, but also when suppliers and builders came to the house. He was forever asking, "Wherever shall we get the money from?" and when he took off on his six-month odysseys (only telling Jo a few days beforehand when he decided to return) he would never leave money to cover the family's needs. Jo would avoid answering the door in case it was a creditor or, even more alarmingly, a real estate agent whom Earle had instructed to sell the house. Other times it would be someone seeking her husband after he had backed into their car or boat and then driven away.

"He didn't praise us as children," said Toni. "He only admired those who shared what he felt was his higher purpose, reserving encouragement for the occasions when we walked on the road he had chosen." It was a route neither child felt inclined or able to take.

Toni escaped to New York as a teenager to became a go-go dancer. She then set up a restaurant with her brother in St. Augustine, Florida (Bill was apparently an excellent cook), where her speciality was to perform flamenco. Briefly married and then divorced, she later took up employment with IBM, becoming a financial operations manager, a job from which she had recently taken early retirement. She told me that she "woke up and smelled the coffee" while still young and so managed to avoid being drawn into the "relentless stress" of her home life.

Bill was a different story. "He wanted to protect my mother," Toni explained. "She had such a tough time when Dad was away. Despite her unqualified love for my father, and he for her, it was very difficult for her to get along alone. Mother also had to explain at the local church why her husband was always absent—although often not knowing where he was—and that hurt her too.

"And what happened to Bill?" I asked. I'd never deduced what had destroyed him, but I was now beginning to suspect the underlying cause.

"Bill was not my father—he had other talents. He was such a kind, gifted and gentle man and I loved him dearly, but he never got encouragement from my father and he so badly needed his endorsement. That, combined with the terrible stress of coping at home with the absences, protecting my mother and the money issues, wore him down."

"Did you see Bill before he died?" I asked, although I felt I was intruding further than was comfortable for both of us. Toni's face was turned from me, and after a few seconds she looked back from the front seat, emotion surfacing through her usual composure.

"Yes, Bill came to live with me in Florida while he was being nursed. Referring to the crushing home responsibilities, there's one thing he told me that I shall never forget. He said it would be 'my turn next.'"

Toni spent the last six months of Earle's life nursing her father. Earle was too ill to travel, and she used the time to get to know him better, recalling a turning point in the last few weeks when he told her, with salvationary simplicity, that she was "all right now"—as if he now rated her value along with that of his other possessions.

"Was it worth the price you had to pay?" I asked as we drove back to the airport.

Toni could not answer this easily. The death of a beloved brother and the stress her mother had to endure hardly made it a fair question either. She conceded that she understood why her father had done what he had, but could not go as far as condoning it. A day later I received an e-mail. Attached was a poem by Earle's mentor as a student, Robert Frost, and she felt that the last verse was the closest thing to justifying his "higher purpose":

> The woods are lovely, dark and deep.
> But I have promises to keep,
> And miles to go before I sleep,
> And miles to go before I sleep.

CHAPTER 2

The Mystery of the Missing Gainsborough

A number of the lots from the Los Angeles art sale looked grimly familiar. Call it trade snobbery or self-preservation, but when a portrait that has previously failed to sell returns to the salesroom it starts to look sickly in the eyes of the art trade. And it's not just the faces. As if sapped of their self-esteem, otherwise noble still lifes start to decompose, religious pictures go gloomy, and even upbeat, sunny landscapes will turn overcast.

Fresh pictures with a new story to tell hum with seductive appeal. And one of them had just beckoned me. It was November 2006, and I had been flipping through a sale catalogue on Bendor's desk and had just come across a small color illustration of a rustic woodland scene with figures. Catalogued "Follower of Salomon van Ruisdael," it had an estimate of $2,000–$3,000.

"Follower" is a bit of a catchall term used by auction houses to describe normally a later artist, of lesser ability, who follows the style of another. Ruisdael was an artist worth following. Something of a celebrity of the seventeenth-century Dutch landscape scene, he was esteemed for his picturesque, well-organized compositions of trees, tranquil waters and gray blue skies. So ideally conceived and constructed were Ruisdael's landscapes that he continued to be in vogue long after his death, giving rise to a group of English followers eager to satisfy their more sophisticated patrons with a touch of continental class.

But this was no normal imitator of the Dutch master. Everything about the illustration triggered positive feelings of familiarity. The composition hit me first. The weaving row of oaks, ashes and beeches, the pool of dark water and the pair of pick-axe-wielding laborers followed a choreography I had seen before. So did the foliage—a melody of light and dark greens held together with a wiry, serpentine mesh of upper branches. Artists who regularly need to create large areas of greenery in landscapes will often develop shorthand, and the fluent strokes and stipples that shaped these woodland trees was instantly recognizable. Great artists are also risk takers; they constantly push the boundaries of illusion, like ambitious magicians. The painter of this wood knew that in certain lights the trunks of beech trees can shine like white metal, reflecting rather than absorbing light.

OK, I thought, relax for a moment. Although this had the look of a master's work, why not a good copyist instead? For a few facile tricks is often all it takes to lure the optimistic. All too often I had been drawn toward the rocks by these sirens and had had countless catalogue and desktop dreams thwarted—mercifully usually before, but occasionally, and most painfully and memorably, after I had committed financially.

I took a deep breath and gazed again at the little image, this time employing as much skepticism as I could muster. Come on, I told myself, seek out the weaknesses, signs of clumsiness, passages of crudeness or deadness; check the figures for their solidity and weight—anything to stop my excitement from dissolving into fantasy. But this exercise only succeeded in achieving the reverse: it allowed me to spot another artistic ruse, more subtle than the shining bark. It consisted of a flashing stroke of creamy-orange pigment on the trunk of an aging, possibly dying, oak tree, a few centimeters from the exact center of the composition. Ostensibly a shaft of sunlight, or freak reflection, it fluoresced like a small swarm of fireflies and lit the orange-browns of the turning leaves above. It was an artistic trick to enliven the glade.

I had found enough sleepers in my life to ration my emotions, but what now affected my breathing was not just the artist, but the subject. Anecdotes relating to Ruisdael's childhood began to flicker. As art dealers we are often asked what mental processes are brought to bear in recognizing a lost or miscatalogued painting: sometimes the trick is as easy as turning over the right card in a game of Memory—unambiguous and satisfyingly instant. On other occasions memories shoot through the dark like distress signals, barely long enough to allow their trajectory to be fixed. This beguiling image was a combination of both. I recognized the artist and the subject, but what was so extraordinary to me at that moment was that this picture existed at all. Where had it been? How could it have missed the sweep of one hundred years of art history?

I dropped the catalogue in front of Bendor.

"You see this little Dutch landscape. Doesn't it remind you of something?" I asked.

Adjusting his glasses, Bendor leaned forward. It took him only a few seconds to realize that he was surveying the familiar contours of *Cornard Wood*.

Thomas (known as Tom) Gainsborough was brought up among the clatter of a huge family. Although early biographical accounts can be contradictory, it appears he was the youngest of four boys; he also had five sisters, and the half-timbered house where he was born in Sudbury, Suffolk, in 1723, would have been filled with as much noise as in its previous incarnation as a coaching inn. How great an influence his father was on England's first great Romantic painter is difficult to measure, but from the account of one biographer he certainly cut a dash. A clothier by trade, the elder Gainsborough, John, was notably tall, wore his hair carefully parted, and was remarkable for the whiteness and regularity of his teeth in an age when many other people's were rotting stumps. He wore a sword in the foppish eighteenth-century manner, and although not recorded as dexterous with a brush, did have a reputation as a mean two-handed fencer. Tom's mother, Mary, née Burroughs, was the sister of a clergyman schoolteacher and was both cultivated and artistically accomplished. Although none of her work has been rediscovered, she is known to have been a painter of flowers and still lifes, and Tom would have been brought up with the smell of turpentine and the sight of his mother amid paintbrushes, fruit and petals; she also actively encouraged his art from an early age. His mother's spirit seems to surface in some of Tom's juvenile portraits, some of which include poetically observed English flora, worn, discarded or placed in the background and testifying to a notably independent sensitivity to the aesthetic impact of wildflowers.

Evocative glimpses of the child prodigy can be gained from early reminiscences. Tom attended the local grammar school, where his mother's brother, Humphrey, was headmaster. Clearly not a conventional academic, Tom demonstrated his natural leanings by adorning the covers of his exercise books with sketches and caricatures that went down so well with some of his schoolmates that they commissioned him to do the same for theirs in return for them doing his academic exercises. Matters came to a head, however, when he used his artistic skills to forge a note from his father to his uncle, the headmaster, saying, "Give Tom a holiday." Initially the forgery worked a treat and he managed to spend the day wandering around with his pencil, sketching scenes and details in the surrounding countryside. Later that day Tom's uncle uncovered the ruse and reported it at once to his father. That evening an extremely distressed John, the businessman in him having a particular horror of forgery, confronted his son, exclaiming that he would one day be hanged for such reprobate behavior. When the boy responded by laying out the sketches, his father's temper changed, he forgave all, and in a mood of elation declared, "Tom will be a genius."

In England up until this date there were three main styles from which a landscape painter could make a living: topographical, which meant delineating a customer's house and land with a portrait painter's precision, possibly even including the occupants themselves as miniature portraits, sometimes on horses or in a coach; classical, for the cosmopolitan Grand Tourist who liked Greek and Roman arcadia and a flash of toga beneath the trees; and mid-seventeenth-century Dutch, particularly favored by the Suffolk business class, who liked their landscape pruned and raked, removed of its menace and conforming to mercantile notions of good order.

Although the young Gainsborough almost always incorporated figures into landscapes, he was not interested in experimenting with classicism at this stage in his life. He was also no jobbing topographer, and although the Dutch and continental painters provided his compositions with a sometimes formulaic structural template, the most impressive imprint on his work was nature itself. The countryside he recorded as a young man—either as stand-alone landscapes or the setting for his portraits—is arrestingly fresh and natural, full of breezy observation to lift the spirit. Stems of corn and barley don't unbendingly stand, they sway; sandy banks, rocks and pools of light riddle the woodland with a naturalist's observation; clouds don't loiter, they scud; the larger trees in particular are animate and expressive—each a separate biography testifying to the artist's deep attachment to a natural rather than a contrived beauty. In his intuitive records of rural Suffolk, the young Gainsborough demonstrated the skills and feelings of an early Romantic poet.

Response on its own was not enough to communicate this, however, and to impart his highly tuned insight he perfected a magical skill rarely practiced with such distinction in England since the death of Van Dyck a century earlier. The process of glazing was highly challenging. It required artists to judge and anticipate the effect of one color glowing through another. An oil painting on canvas or panel requires a base of underpaint before the artist can embark on the work. This normally acts as little more than an appropriate surface upon which to apply the brushstrokes, although it will provide warmth and body to the final paint layers. The consummate glazer, however, allows underpaint (in Gainsborough's case it could vary from orange to pinky-beige) to partly shine through. Gainsborough's top pigments tended toward transparency, sometimes with unusual added ingredients like ground glass, increasing the possibilities for the depth, mood and refinement that glazing can achieve. When Gainsborough was presented for the first time with a fiddle, it is documented that he became professionally proficient on it in days: the most potent way of expressing his particular brand of suffusing one tone through another is to liken it to the complexity of eighteenth-century musical harmony.

Around the age of fourteen, after his talents were recognized, Tom left Sudbury for long spells in London, entering an apprenticeship with Hubert Gravelot, a decorative painter and designer of European stature, and later studying with the leading portrait and genre painter Francis Hayman. He rapidly developed his art, thirstily absorbing the opportunities of a cosmopolitan city. In his early twenties, after returning to East Anglia to live and work in Ipswich, he launched himself on the city of Bath, where society congregated to take the waters, parade, cross-pollinate and be painted. Within a few years he was the most successful portrait painter in England, sharing the honor with his near-contemporary Sir Joshua Reynolds. Landscape remained his first love, however, and one painting above all others, which he completed in 1748 while living and working in Ipswich before settling in Bath, monumentalized this proclivity. Looking back on its extraordinary commercial success, Gainsborough noted toward the end of his life that the work had passed through the hands of twenty dealers, and at one point in this feverish cycle he had bought it back himself, for nineteen guineas. Appropriately, it now hangs in the National Gallery, where it can be admired in the context of some of Europe's greatest masterpieces, demonstrating just how proficient the boy from Sudbury had become by around twenty years of age.

It is a large canvas, about four feet high and five feet across, and although Gainsborough self-deprecatingly described it as not one of his "riper performances" and having "little idea of composition," it is a ravishing panorama of detail and atmosphere. The subject portrayed is a wood, its glades and clearings scattered with little incidents. A rustic is digging marl and making eyes at his seated female lover; another figure gathers wood; ducks are lifting from the water, a pair of donkeys exchange companionable looks, and, as an escape for the eye, through the center of the wood runs a path; at the end of it, in the dim distance, and toward which a traveler is walking, can be seen the spire of a church. The picture's scale, detail and expansive composition, combined with Gainsborough's relish for the recording of trees, make it one of the rustic masterpieces of the National Gallery, a painting never out of fashion, illustrated, referred to and studied since it first left the artist's studio more than 250 years earlier. It has two names. One is *Gainsborough's Forest,* as befitted the artist's momentous artistic achievement, but latterly it also came to be known by its location. This is a dense patch of wood in a neighboring parish a few miles from the artist's boyhood home, a walk of less than an hour culminating in a long and gentle slope. In Gainsborough's day it was common land where villagers could freely graze their cattle, forage for firewood and walk. Its name is Cornard Wood.

I t was three days before the sale and I woke up with thoughts of Cornard Wood pulsating through my head. The previous evening Bendor and I had taken a closer look at the picture on his screen (most auction houses post their pictures online) and although I had not been able to determine its condition, we were now as convinced as we could be of two things: it was an early work by Thomas Gainsborough—how early was difficult to establish at this stage—and, although more than half the size of the National Gallery picture, with fewer figures and less detail and drama, it was definitely of Cornard Wood. Although the composition was narrower, lacking trees and a slope on the left, it was also undoubtedly painted from the same viewpoint.

Remarkably, the emergence of this new image suggested that the National Gallery's monument of English landscape painting was not unique, that Gainsborough, either before or after he had painted his early masterpiece, had painted this. That was thrilling in itself, but it raised the burning questions of why and when. Hard-bitten experience has shown me that you need a cogent argument to launch a new claim, particularly when dealing with the big names, and if we were going to represent this to the art world as a newly discovered Gainsborough it had to be understood and placed within the context of the artist's development. Find the missing pieces and we had the potential to turn an anonymous Dutch landscape, five thousand miles from home in Los Angeles, into a footnote in British landscape history.

On this type of occasion the day's agenda sets itself. Bendor dropped everything to read all published material on *Cornard Wood* in particular anything that might include a reference to another painting of the same title. Given the picture's celebrity, the task would be substantial. In the meantime I canceled appointments and headed off in search of an extremely scarce memoir of Gainsborough. It had been hurriedly written shortly after he died, in 1789, and, although created for the author's personal advancement and to back up an implausible claim that he had discovered the artist, it was known to include some valuable fragmentary remarks about Gainsborough's early work.

The author, Philip Thicknesse, went from being an apothecary to a marine lieutenant in Jamaica, where he engaged in warfare with escaped slaves. He was malevolent and argumentative, once even imprisoned for libeling an army colonel, and in 1754 achieved respectability by purchasing the post of lieutenant governor of Landguard Fort at Felixstowe, a day's walk from where Gainsborough was based in Ipswich. For rare books such as this the National Art Library—the country's greatest collection of art books—is one of the few places you can be sure to find a copy.

Having long been assisted by professional researchers, the last time I had visited the library was ten years earlier, and I had forgotten the excitement that even inanimate buildings can engender when quarry has been scented, the chase has begun, and there is the prospect of finding transformative answers in books and records. This great resource is located on the first floor of the Victoria and Albert Museum in South Kensington, and as I scaled the imposing granite steps at 10 A.M. I felt a touch of adrenaline. At the same time I could not help but be encouraged by the row of sculptured artistic worthies along the façade, among whom, palette in hand, was Thomas Gainsborough himself, stonily oblivious to my quest on his behalf.

The library's main reading room is cavernous, its lofty walls of red spines and mahogany shelves dully lit by discolored overhead skylights. It is an academic cathedral of leather, cloth and polished wood of a type that is found (on a much smaller scale) in ancient London clubs. Halfway up the walls runs a continuous wrought-iron gallery; a level below a series of bronze and terra-cotta busts of historical luminaries gaze out across the readers, who are silently seated in numbered compartments along a chain of joined mahogany writing desks. Most of the readers around me looked young, casual and studentlike, acolytes of the world of academic art history to which I myself had belonged at university, and it reminded me how big an industry art history has become. The innumerable articles, books, lectures, theses and doctorates testify to this, and every time a piece of scholarship is procreated, a new or known artist's work is emphasized or further classified. When this essence is fed into the thinking of museums and collectors it can create market demand. It is also pivotal to the process of sleuthing works of art. As a painting can only be deemed lost if it is seen as worth missing, the process of making discoveries is reliant on this alchemy of academia: it establishes status, provides evidence and underpins value.

A young librarian standing behind the central desk showed me how to complete the form, and when it came to filling in the book title he looked up.

"Funny that, for a rare book," he said. "You're the second person this week to ask for it."

Here we go, I thought with a silent groan.

Often the only way you know that others are onto a sleeper is the evidence of activities similar to your own. I could recall with pained lucidity the occasion a rare sculpture purportedly from Westminster Hall came up in a country sale with barely a day's lead time. I asked my researcher to go to the London Library to seek out any books on the subject. Half an hour later he telephoned me from the library in dismay: the shelf was bare—all relevant titles had been loaned out the previous day to another member. It left us flailing in the dark, powerless to bid when the work was offered for sale the next morning. Business paranoia now returning, I asked myself: why had someone else asked for so obscure a book on Gainsborough only a few days earlier? The librarian could not or would not tell me any more.

I was directed to the invigilation area, a segregated zone for the library's bibliographic treasures where the seated invigilator—on this shift it was a middle-aged female librarian with pendulous glasses—has the task of watching over the readers of the more valuable books. As books are stored outside the library I was aware that I had forty-five minutes to wait under her owl gaze and used the time to respond to e-mails on my BlackBerry.

One message was from Bendor. He had gone off to the Witt Library to research further, but said he had dropped some books on my desk. "Read the letter from Gainsborough," he added as a rather gnomic sign-off. Another e-mail had come in the previous evening from the auction house, who at our request had promptly sent some close-up digital images of the picture, a standard service provided by most auction houses to prospective bidders. However, the speed with which they had supplied them suggested to me that we were not the first to ask, which added to my unease. The images were too small to usefully download from my small screen, and I would have to wait until I was back in front of our gallery screens.

Almost an hour had passed when the book was placed before me. Smaller and thinner than I expected, it was bound in the library's standard red cloth and it immediately struck me how well suited this natty publication was to being pressed into the hands of targeted acquaintances—Thicknesse's quick-fix social passport to cultural distinction in late-eighteenth-century society. I gingerly turned back the crisp, laid-paper title page, wondering who had been here so recently. The type was bold and old-fashioned, with s's in the form of f's, and it took a few minutes to calibrate the punctuation and style. I decided to leave the opening section till last, and began by attempting to speed-read the other four-fifths of the book, but after ten minutes I found myself mired in Georgian verbiage, much of it concerning Gainsborough's reluctance to get round to painting Thicknesse's portrait, while the rest was tiresomely self-serving, the author's transparent attempt to go down in history as a noble benefactor and patron of the artist.

I turned to the beginning and after a few pages I was rewarded with a sentence that bolted off the page. The words, which I had seen quoted in abridged form in later biographies, referred to Gainsborough's defining love for his home surroundings. But seeing them now in their entirety, enshrined in

Thicknesse's memoir, I realized they were describing something more significant—what could be called Gainsborough's
photographic memory for nature:

> Though he had no idea of becoming a painter then, yet there
> was not a picturesque clump of trees, nor even a single tree
> of beauty no, nor hedgerow, stone, or post, at the corner of
> lanes, for some miles around the place of his nativity, that he
> had not so perfectly in his mind's eye, that had he known he
> could use a pencil, he could have perfectly delineated.

Needless to say, the lines were in conjunction with something
that showed Thicknesse in a favorable light—a group of drawings, many of them of trees, that Gainsborough had executed in
later boyhood and that Thicknesse had had the implicit judgment and good taste to buy from him. The author described
them as jottings from nature done on "slips of paper" and "old
dirty letters," and they immediately put me in mind of the
sketches that Gainsborough might have done that day he played
truant. Among them was what Thicknesse described as Gainsborough's "first effort," which he esteemed beyond the others:
"The first effort . . . is a group of trees now in my possession and
they are such as would not be unworthy of a place at this day in
one of his best landscapes . . . lots of other tree sketches too."
I scribbled the quotations down and continued to trawl for
further references, but there was little else to garner from the
author's account of Gainsborough's very early days, which concluded with how he went "very young" to London. Although
there had been no dramatic revelations, it had gotten me thinking,

and as I made my way out of the museum—hardly registering half a millennium of some of the finest European sculpture en route to the doors—I continued to reflect on the artist's remarkable productivity as a child. One thing was clearer. According to Thicknesse, a decade or so before he painted *Cornard Wood* Gainsborough had harbored an intense interest in the picturesque possibilities of trees, which he had obviously encountered in abundance either "singly" or in "groups" or "clumps" around Sudbury. Seen another way, the artistic thought process that culminated in his great landscape at the age of about twenty had begun when he was a youngster.

My professional library began thirty years ago when I bought my first dictionary of artists—an art dealer's stock in trade—while I was dealing between Liverpool and Chester shortly before I left for university, and since then it has grown piecemeal, biographies, catalogues raisonnés and exhibition catalogues together forming a fit-for-purpose engine room of business. Most simple questions can be answered with a quick flick through our publications on British portrait and landscape (some now worn and grubby from frenetic use), the subjects that are the gallery's main, but far from sole, focus. The library also doubles as Bendor's office, and given that he initially organized the shelving when we moved in a year earlier, and did so partly to suit his own working methods as well as his own height—he is six foot four while I am five feet ten and a half inches on a good day—I pretty soon accepted the futility of trying to find books in there on my own.

Which was why I was so pleased to find deposited on my

desk the book I had intended to go to next. Entitled *The Letters of Thomas Gainsborough*, it was the last work of scholarship on the artist by Dr. John Hayes, a friend of mine who had died a year earlier at the age of seventy-three. John and I had had many lunches together at the Arts Club and the Garrick Club, and Gainsborough was always on the agenda. He had written copiously on his beloved artist, including a formidable two-volume work on all his landscape paintings, becoming in the process as good an authority on a single historical figure as a biographer can be. He had served as director of both the Museum of London and the National Portrait Gallery, and during his retirement continued to curate international exhibitions on Gainsborough with punctilious scholarship.

The book in question was a compilation of 147 letters and documents in the artist's own hand, starting from his early twenties. John had added a brief biography, his usual sharp insight and in some cases Gainsborough's portraits of the recipients. As I sat down at my desk to read the letter that Bendor had marked with a yellow sticker, I had a momentary tinge of sadness that John was not around to collaborate with me at this exciting moment. He had been invaluable a year earlier when I had discovered a missing version of Gainsborough's *The Cottage Door* in a New York sale, and he liked nothing better than anointing a new work, even when it meant revising his earlier writing—an openness not shared by all art historians. This new contender would have captivated him.

Bendor had drawn a bold blue arrow on the sticker pointing to letter number 104, dated March 11, 1788. It was written by Gainsborough the year he died and addressed to the Reverend Henry Bate Dudley, proprietor and editor of the *Morning Herald*.

He was responding to a query about the circumstances surrounding his painting of *Cornard Wood* (forty years after he had painted it). The most startling line, and the one where Bendor's arrow point fell, was the following: "This picture was actually painted in Sudbury, in the year 1748: it was begun before I left school;—and was the means of my father sending me to London."

I knew there had been academic conjecture on the exact date of *Cornard Wood*, partly (and this I had forgotten) because of a rogue line—the one I had just read—by the sixty-year-old artist looking back to his youth. Although Gainsborough had clearly recalled the execution date as 1748, in the same sentence he contradicted himself by saying that it "was begun before I left school" and was "the means of my father sending me to London." As it is generally accepted that he left school for London at the age of around fourteen it implied—bizarrely—that it took five years to paint. Furthermore, on the basis of style, *Cornard Wood* belongs to a group of works that he painted in the late 1740s—breezy, silvery and slightly French in spirit.

That evening Bendor and I sat adhered to his superior screen, his cursor hovering over every centimeter of the image, zooming in on details. The amount of ink that has been expended on the subject of Gainsborough's landscapes meant that Bendor had been book-bound for most of the day and only now had been able to apprise me of his findings. As we digitally luxuriated in the picture I began to weigh the options and muddle through the scenarios.

It was of course possible that Gainsborough's memory was playing tricks on him, that he had confused his dates and that the whole picture was executed in 1748—he was, after all, recollecting an event that had happened at least forty years earlier and he might just have forgotten. But the letter sounded too precise for this and there was also no evidence that Gainsborough's mind was slipping at this date. So I then tried taking the words literally, devoid of any interpretation: what if the picture had indeed taken five years to paint—that he had perhaps acquired the canvas as a child at school, mapped out the composition, and then gradually completed it? I did not like this either, partly because it would have been most unusual for a schoolboy to paint a canvas five feet wide but also, more persuasively, because the picture had been analyzed by the National Gallery and there was no sign of its having been painted in stages (with analysis and testing it is not overly complicated to determine if a painting has had a protracted evolution). For a work of this size to have taken over five years it would have been inconceivable for it not to have been painted in interludes, each new layer or addition overlaying or at least partly overlapping, an earlier one. The National Gallery's prodigiously equipped conservation department would have been quick to detect these different stages had they taken place. It also occurred to me that if the painting was the "means of my father sending me to London," it would have had to have had impact—and therefore to have been largely completed in some form when he left for London at around fourteen.

I then turned to the most convincing hypothesis of all, and for different reasons the National Gallery's curators had gone some way to proposing it themselves. Bendor had copied down their label beneath the painting, in which they had suggested—no doubt with Gainsborough's letter in mind—that *Cornard Wood* may have been based on earlier sketches. I let this thought percolate for a few minutes, allowing the variant implications to suggest themselves. The Gallery seemed to be raising the idea that "began" referred not to the moment he embarked on the big canvas but the moment he started thinking and working toward the idea. In light of what I had been reading this sounded entirely plausible. Were not Thicknesse's juvenile sketches exactly the sort of artwork that might have erupted from this process? But if this were the case, why not take the idea one stage further? For the work to have been sufficiently impressive for it to become the *means*—financial or otherwise—by which the Sudbury boy orbited onto the London scene it was likely to be more than mere sketches. A far more probable scenario surely was that young Tom had done something dramatically indicative of his genius, and if this were the case, why should he not have employed a skill that we are led to believe he had been taught by his mother at a young age? Why could he not have produced an oil painting, a work of startling precocity that became not just his passport to London but the first stage toward his rural masterpiece?

When you buy a painting at auction from abroad it takes four weeks or more for the moment of revelation when, as the picture is unscrewed from the crate or cut from its bubble packaging, the truth is fully revealed beneath the ruthless glare of gallery lighting.

Deciding what to pay for a painting that we have not seen in the flesh is a perilous business, but one we have become increasingly used to. Looking back over the past three years of computer-screen art buying I would estimate a statistical hit rate of seven out of eight. A hit is something commercially resaleable, ranging from a major sleeper—which can return a great multiple of the purchase price—to the close shave, which is basically a disappointment, but one on which, by judicious placing in another auction, we can probably get our money back. The miss is best defined as the unmitigated cock-up. It usually involves buying a picture that we have assessed from digital images on our screen to be the real thing, but which on arrival turns out to be either in ruinous condition or, as has happened a number of times, a cunning copy (on one occasion a picture even turned out to be a glorified painted photo). The hideous specter of the cock-up naturally has the tendency to curb excessive commitment.

Looking at the digital image on my screen with twenty-four hours to go, I now had to start the thought process. It was impossible for either myself or Bendor to get out to Los Angeles on short notice, so it was going to have to be the usual game of long-distance risk. If this turned out to be a work of quality and in good condition, given what we now knew about its likely function it would be worth £400,000. If it turned out to be a late copy, a mere £1,000. The problem with a screen is getting a grip on the painting's physical properties. Buying art through a computer is like trying to taste with a cold. An oil painting is in fact a three-dimensional object, its surface texture representing an important part of its age, authenticity and allure, and even though a good digital image or a detail can offer tremendous clarity, it cannot impart the full feeling and taste of an encounter in the flesh. We did not know anything about the picture's history and how it got to America, facts which would have assisted our thoughts about whether it could be a recent fake. The auction house had covered itself entirely with the term "Follower": if it transpired to have been knocked out in the past three weeks, they would not be obliged to return our money, so there was no comfort there. John Hayes's landscape volumes had come up with a record of a "variant copy" of *Cornard Wood* in a collection in Utah. Was this, I now asked myself, the same picture? If so, it was unlikely that Hayes had seen it in the flesh, and possible that he would have been working from a black-and-white photograph. That would have compromised his judgment and so would not have concerned me. But what if he had seen it in the flesh and deemed it an obvious copy?

I had one more port of call, and I followed my last lead the next day, the morning of the sale. An obvious question that would hover over this picture if we bought it would be, how could a fourteen-year-old boy be more accomplished than most other artists would become in their whole adult careers? Or, put another way, what proof was there that Gainsborough was painting so young? Although it was not a question that personally worried me—juvenile genius was a phenomenon I had observed in other painters—it would be brandished by the incredulous. There was one woman, however, who had addressed the same issue a thousand times, and she was in my gallery that morning.

Adrienne Corri has had a mixed reception in the art world. She first came to my notice when she made the amazing discovery of an early self-portrait painted by Gainsborough at twelve or thirteen. I subsequently managed to buy it and was able to take it home for two years before the need for funds prompted its return to my gallery for resale. Immediately afterward it was exhibited at the Tate Gallery in a major Gainsborough retrospective, causing wonder and admiration for his certainty of characterization and skillful deployment of glaze at so young an age. The first moment I spotted the Los Angeles landscape, that little face in the beguiling self-portrait came to mind, and it had remained with me over the past forty-eight hours.

John Hayes had admitted to me that he was a little bit scared of Adrienne, an actress turned amateur art historian who shook the trees of Gainsborough scholarship in the early 1980s with a combination of relentless research and confrontational vigor. He was not alone in his trepidation. But John added that what she had uncovered could not be ignored and he acknowledged that the self-portrait was a revelation. For her part this petite, dynamic Scotswoman, who introduced Sean Connery to the game of golf while she was married to the actor Daniel Massey, was a little more forgiving at the age of seventy-seven when I contacted her at home than she had been on her first forays into the field.

Adrienne Corri first took on Gainsborough scholars in the late 1970s, when she attempted to prove that a portrait of the actor David Garrick in the Alexandra Theatre, in Birmingham, was by the young Gainsborough. This was a diversion from her life as a serious actress, which had begun at fourteen and included innumerable stage, television and film parts, ranging from Desdemona at the Old Vic to Mena in *Doctor Who*.

She took to her new role of art sleuth with the distinction of a leading lady, having developed a burning desire to prove that

Gainsborough could have painted Garrick when only sixteen, as per corresponding to the likely date of that portrait. Her case was built on a throwaway line by an eighteenth-century politician that a Mr. Fonnereau of Ipswich gave young Gainsborough his "first chance," by lending him £300. This led to the most arduous part of her odyssey, which was to try to find a bank record to prove it. It took her a year just to gain access to the archives of the Bank of England, but in retrospect that was the easy part. She went on to discover that eighteenth-century banks ran a hideously arcane system by which account holders did not have their bills paid directly by their bank but via smaller, merchant banks that acted as intermediaries. At the Bank of England, ten ledgers recording these intermediary loans were in use at any one time, making the linking of payer to payee a Sisyphean task.

The whole project lasted six years. She tracked down ledgers from many other banks, including Hoare's, Drummonds, Barclays and the National Westminster. At that time there were no photocopiers, so she ended up filling thirty-six books with notes. Her findings, which she published in the art world's eminent journal *Burlington Magazine*, coupled with her unswerving conviction of their implications, were so controversial that they caused art historians to take deep fright: she claimed that Gainsborough was receiving very substantial payments from the age of ten. Up until now, apart from owning the self-portrait, I did not have much reason to engage with this claim. This little landscape had changed all that.

"What I established was as a direct result of what I found," Adrienne enunciated over the telephone in her powerful actress's diction. "You can go and see it yourself in the archives. The Handley account at the Bank of England indicates that the first money from Fonnereau to Gainsborough was in 1736—when he was ten years old."

"How much?" I asked.

"The hefty sum of £300," she replied briskly. "The same figure referred to by the politician. The money continues to be paid for the next twenty years, but from 1739 it seems to have been invested."

"Why then?"

"I'm not sure," she said, "but 1739 is when Claude Fonnereau died and Gainsborough went to London. That may be significant. In 1750 a large proportion was withdrawn. This may well have had something to do with his father's death and his move to Ipswich around that time."

We talked for half an hour. At full tilt even on the phone Adrienne Corri was formidable, and I could see how art historians would have run for cover. Her argument was vulnerable because the work she had done was exhaustingly arcane and not easily verifiable; it required someone else to exactly replicate her research in order to properly engage, but to date no one has, which meant that her deductions had to be accepted—or, in her case, most often rejected—at face value. Others have argued against her that if Gainsborough had been making £300 per year he would have gone to London not as a humble apprentice, but as a prince (although Adrienne would argue that it could easily have been held in trust).

By the time I put the receiver down, after mentioning coyly that I hoped to have something to show her soon, I knew what

John had meant. Adrienne's findings cannot be ignored: there is much more to the story of young Tom than we may ever know.

"So do you specialize in anything particular?" asked the good-looking lady seated on my left at a dinner party that evening.

It is a frequent follow-up question when, at a first meeting, you reveal yourself to be an art dealer. I have a fluent, forever evolving answer. It starts with a reference to paintings of the human face—my stock in trade—and then spreads to cover my latest enthusiasm, or what I guess might be theirs. Tonight, however, I was too much on edge for gentle dialogue.

"Well," I said, "in the next half hour in California I'm hoping to buy the painting that revealed the boy Gainsborough to be a genius." Go for broke, I thought, and qualify yourself later.

Pausing a second or two to digest my unexpected salvo, she responded with unexpected skepticism. "Prove it," she said tartly.

So I began to tell her the whole story, starting from the beginning, leaving out very little. One of the reasons why I (and other dealers) sometimes enthusiastically download details of imminent purchases to strangers is that it allows us to hear and test our buying rationale. I have a tendency to become commercially blinkered by the latest obsession, sometimes forgetting the picture-buying public on whom I rely. I take the view that if I cannot sell it to someone's imagination at this stage then I am hardly likely to be able to do so when it is hanging on my gallery wall.

Although the dinner party was being given by Tara Williams,

an art-world hostess, there were no other dealers within earshot I could recognize. In any event I am always careful to withhold crucial facts about an auction house's name or cataloguing details—key words that could be later googled and linked with the picture in question. I also had the warm feeling that we were as prepared as we could be: the bowstring had been drawn, the arrow was in place and I had as good as let loose across the Atlantic. A telephone line had been booked with the auction house, and they had confirmed it in a fax. My gallery manager, Emma Henderson, had checked with me our dollar holdings and which of our bank accounts we were to use; these vary according to the amount and length of time the money is held. Bendor, whom the auctioneers had been instructed to phone for the bid, had arranged to stay late and was waiting in the gallery. My cell phone sat between my legs, discreetly turned to vibrate as backup if they could not reach Bendor. And as a third string, if all else failed, Lottie Tate, another member of my staff was waiting by her phone on a farm in Lincolnshire.

Despite all this, ten minutes into relating the story of the young Gainsborough to my dinner partner, I started to feel anxious. Some of the smaller auction houses are not the efficient organizations they aspire to be and disasters do happen, particularly on sale days. The bidding staff, whose job it is to relay your phone bid to the auctioneer, sometimes fail to contact you, or with maniacal persistence repeatedly try the automatic fax line as you helplessly look on. It has also been known for the in-house electrical system, taxed by the day's excessive requirements, to collapse at the *moment critique* when the auctioneer turns on his microphone to call the room to order—causing the phone systems to die with it. International lines can become engaged, digits can be misread, instructions lost, and all these misadventures, at some time or another, have befallen us. On one occasion a salesroom in Boston chose to telephone both Bendor (the backup bidder) and me in different parts of London at the same time and we ended up unwittingly bidding against each other. The auctioneer was delighted: his Jane Stuart portrait of George Washington, estimated at $2,000–$3,000, made a record sum of $25,000—and we were the only bidders. Fortunately we later got him to cancel the sale and re-offer it, and we bought it for $4,000.

But it is the lost opportunities that really cut deep, not least because the auction house is not legally liable if they forget or do not manage to contact you. I once organized with a California auction house to bid in the middle of the night (British time) on a glorious, miscatalogued Sir Henry Raeburn portrait of a child. I rose the next morning with the sick realization that no one had telephoned. As the day progressed we pieced together the reason. An intern at the auction house, despite been given a fax clearly requesting that I be telephoned on my home number (which was boldly typed on the page), instead chose to telephone the number of our gallery printed beneath our company name; he tried to call the gallery five times, and by playing back the office answering machine we were able to listen to his increasingly desperate, dim-witted bleats for someone to pick up in the early hours of the morning. About one in fifteen of our telephone bids ends in calamity.

I was also concerned about the level. Weighing up the possible downsides, as I had just had a particularly expensive mistake from a sale in New York, I had told Bendor to bid no more than $110,000 including commission. If it turned out to be a

Rembrandt van Rijn (1606–1669), *Rembrandt Laughing*

OIL ON COPPER • 9.35 X 6.69" • 23.75 X 17CM

Catalogued as being by a follower of the great artist and estimated at a mere $2,000–4,000, this small painting caused a sensation when it sold for $5.2 million in a provincial sale in England in October 2007 and was later authenticated as a lost Rembrandt. It subsequently resurfaced in the art press at a valuation of around $40 million.

Thomas Gainsborough (1727–1788), *Portrait of a Gentleman*

OIL ON CANVAS • 25 ¾ X 19" • 65.5 X 48 CM

This painting appeared on eBay without being recognized as the work of Gainsborough. For all the distinction of the head, the overpainted body was ludicrously solid, giving the portrait the overall appearance of a pub sign. It sold for less than $200.

Beneath the heavy overpainting, cleaning and restoration revealed the signature strokes of the jaunty Ipswich-period Gainsborough.

William Dobson (1611–1646),
Portrait of King Charles I (detail)
OIL ON CANVAS • 19 X 15 ½" • 48.3 X 39.4CM

Taken in the middle of the cleaning process, this photograph demonstrates how dirty, ingrained varnish can disguise the defining subtleties of a great artist's work. So obscuring was the varnish layer here that a historic portrait by Dobson was described by the auction house as a copy.

Museum of the Americas

The author and Earle Newton in 1992 with one of the hundreds of portraits—this one attributed to John Riley—that, to my amazement, he had stashed away in a disused church in rural Vermont. The collection I encountered that day in Newton's "Museum of the Americas" has since been fully catalogued and is now on display at the Savannah College of Art and Design in Georgia.

A rural portrait gallery

Tucked away in a village in Vermont, this simple wooden church housed Earle Newton's breathtaking cache of British and American portraits.

William Hogarth (1697–1764), *Lady in Rose Taffeta*

By far the most important and valuable painting in Earle Newton's unusual gallery, this masterly work by England's greatest portrait painter of the period had been picked up by the collector for just $250 thirty or so years earlier. Encountering this picture alone justified my transatlantic pilgrimage.

Thomas Gainsborough (1727–1788),
Self-portrait as a Boy

OIL ON PAPER ON CANVAS • 9 X 8" • 22.8 X 20.3CM

Even as a child Gainsborough possessed prodigious
talent, as indicated by this assured self-portrait, which
probably dates from 1739, the year before he left Sudbury
for London.

Thomas
Gainsborough
(1727–1788),
Cornard Wood

OIL ON CANVAS • 48 X 61"
• 122 X 155 CM

The National
Gallery's *Cornard
Wood*, one of
the most famous
of Gainsborough's
early works, is
an undisputed
masterpiece.
According to the
artist, it changed
hands twenty times
throughout his life.

Thomas Gainsborough (1727–1788), *Cornard Wood*
(pre-restoration)

OIL ON CANVAS • 25 X 30" • 63.5 X 76 CM

In our deliberations about this work, described by the auction house as
being by a "follower of Jacob van Ruisdael," the seventeenth-century
Dutch landscape painter, we had only the catalogue and digital images
to work from. However, the composition and observable technique left
us in little doubt that this was in fact an early work by Gainsborough,
so we resolved to acquire it.

Thomas Gainsborough
(1727–1788), *Cornard
Wood* (post-restoration)

OIL ON CANVAS •
25 X 30" • 63.5 X 76 CM

The subtle glazes and
tones, all hallmarks of
the artist's landscape
technique, are now more
readily seen.

Bohemia in Arlington

Dressed for the 1955 street fair in Arlington, Vermont, are (left to right) Norman Rockwell, Don Trachte, Frank Hall, Vic Donahue and George Hughes.

Norman Rockwell (1897–1978), *The Girl with a Black Eye*

Don Trachte acted as a model for Rockwell. Here he poses as a school principal, peering through the door and preparing for the arrival of a naughty student.

Don Trachte (1915–2005) after Norman Rockwell, *Breaking Home Ties*

OIL ON CANVAS • 44 X 44" • 111.8 X 111.8CM

This painting, a fake, hung in the Norman Rockwell Museum in Stockbridge, with only one determined doubter, until the original was discovered in Trachte's home by his son a year after his death.

Norman Rockwell (1897–1978), *Breaking Home Ties*

OIL ON CANVAS • 44 X 44" • 111.8 X 111.8CM

A side-by-side comparison of the two paintings reveals the original to posses an authority that the copy lacks. The perspective is more convincing, the figures have more weight and presence, and the pigment is more densely worked and applied.

Norman Rockwell (1897–1978), *Breaking Home Ties*

Artfully concealed behind homemade paneling, this poignant work lay hidden for decades until its dramatic discovery by Don Trachte's two sons.

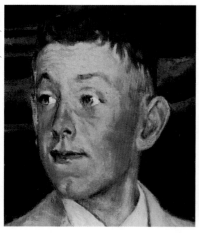

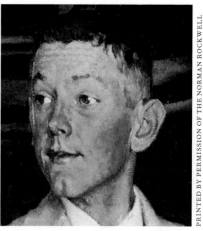

By comparing the boy's head in the two pictures it is possible to identify the shortfalls in quality that reveal Trachte's picture to be a fake. The expression is less alert, details such as the treatment of his ear and mouth are too soft and the overall cast of the features hints at caricature.

Don Trachte (1915–2005) after Norman Rockwell, *Breaking Home Ties* (detail)

Norman Rockwell (1897–1978), *Breaking Home Ties* (detail)

copy, or in a very poor state, it would be unpleasant, but not the bloodbath it would be if we had paid six or seven times that amount. But now, hearing my own sales pitch over the dinner table, I realized I had made a mistake. I started to dwell on the librarian's throwaway reference to the person who had sought the same rare book. Although I could count on one hand the likely dealers who would be able to work out what the picture really was, if they shared our convictions there was no room for risk taking. I began to berate myself. I always have a tendency to give those who are bidding on my behalf a lower level than I would pay myself. In the smoke and heat of commercial conflict I have been known to take the price twice more than I had strategically planned. There is normally a reason when a picture takes off in this way, and I have rarely regretted it.

So, given the picture's prospective importance, why the hell was I not doing the bid myself?

Spurring my misgivings was also the fact that my companion was impressed. It may have been the candlelight, but her eyes were shining as I brought her back to the twenty-first century.

"And now I am sitting waiting for the gallery to give me the news," I said, concluding my story, "and talking to you."

"What a thrilling discovery!" she said almost hoarsely, entirely rid of her former skepticism. "I do hope you get it."

"Sorry to butt in, but I couldn't help overhearing the last bit. It sounds remarkable. When did you first see it?" A gamine blonde in pearls sitting opposite, who had stopped talking to her partner, had joined in.

Now that the landscape's allure was spreading across the table my agitation grew. Discovery of any kind appears to interest people, but this was the first time I had appreciated the emotive power of my newest hunch: if my conjectures were right, when else in my career would I have the opportunity to find so critical a work, the very first work in a great artist's career? I resolved to get Bendor to raise the bid substantially as soon I could artfully extricate myself from the table, which was looking difficult as the conversation had turned to the ethics of art dealing and I found myself in the dock. Now the man two seats down, married to my shiny-eyed dinner partner, waded in.

"Let's face it, like me you do your job for one primary reason: to make money." I noticed a touch of mockery as he shot a grin at his wife. "Art is a commodity, and you dealers are just experts at talking it up," he added for good measure, looking to the table for support.

Wearily, for this was not the first time I'd had to cope with such onslaughts, I obligingly responded.

"That may be true, but it can be the by-product that really gets you out of bed in the morning. For me, money is the evidence you have gotten something right: and in the case of a lost picture the proof that you have salvaged something of significance." Ouch, I thought, does that sound a touch too worthy? Too bad if it did; I was in a hurry to exit, and anyway this man was annoying me.

At that moment my seat vibrated. Snatching the phone to my ear and apologetically catching the eye of our hostess, I withdrew from the fray and clumsily made for the sanctuary of the kitchen with the phone to my ear.

"You can sack me if you want," said Bendor in a notably assured voice on the other end.

My God, I thought. He has failed to bid. This was another

reason telephone buying goes wrong. Human error. The bidder goes to the loo, is distracted, or plain forgets to take the auction house's call.

"What do you mean?" I said in an urgent whisper so as not to be overheard by the table.

"The picture made approximately one hundred and twenty all in—ten thousand more than the limit," he said with the same impassivity.

My worst fear now rose from the mire. I had not given him enough. How profoundly stupid was that?

"Now, taking today's rate of exchange," he added in a higher octave, "that's not as bad as it sounds."

Bad for whom, I thought. And anyway, why tell me this now?

"So who bought it?" I fretted, staring down at the tiled kitchen floor.

"That's what I mean," said Bendor. "Fire me if you will. I took it on. *We* bought it."

Thinking about it later, I don't think he had any intention of sticking to my limit anyway.

We were all in our weekly meeting when the doorbell sounded and the picture was delivered. Although it had been paid for and picked up from the auction house two weeks earlier, it had taken a fortnight to be crated, make its way across to New York, be flown across the Atlantic, clear customs and then be driven from the airport to Dover Street. Every Monday at 11 A.M. we meet to plan the week and review the previous one, and by sheer coincidence we had been discussing the

Gainsborough only minutes earlier. News had reached us that the underbidder had been Andrew Wyld, a distinguished Bond Street dealer specializing in early English drawings, and the view around the table was that if you were going to end up paying fifty times the lower estimate, there were few better dealers to force you up there. The picture had already been uncrated but was swathed in paper and bubble packaging, and Bendor and I both moved in to finish the task. We cut and tore at it using scissors and fingers, and as we did so I got my first glimpse of the corner of a carved and gilded period frame. A good start, I thought—just the sort of mid-eighteenth-century carved and gilded centers and corners style you might expect. The next foretaste, as we peeled away more wrapping, was a flash of green foliage from beneath a tear of brown paper. Even better, I now felt, noticing a telltale swipe of glaze on its fringes. Struggling to pull off the Scotch tape, Bendor then turned the frame on its front to fully remove the final layer. Its dusty underside now revealed, amid the scribbled chalk auction numbers and backing paper, we saw a printed label, scraped and torn. We craned forward. It was for the London art dealers Agnew's; who have been trading since 1817. Beneath the company logo was some faded ink writing. *"Cornard Wood,"* it read.

The back of a picture will often give you more information than the front ever can. Dealers, collectors and inventory makers often marked up the backs of paintings with brief descriptive details, and half the time those inscriptions remain in place. Some years earlier I had bought at a sale in Vienna a portrait painted on plaster believed to represent a continental king or emperor. With the aid of my then researcher we had worked out that it corresponded to a portrait of Charles II by Antonio Verrio, a visiting

Italian artist, from the ceiling of St. George's Hall, Windsor Castle, a building thought to have been entirely destroyed by George IV. It involved considerable research and sourcing of an image in watercolor taken of the ceiling before it was pulled down, and then developing a hypothesis of how this fragment might have been preserved (we think the architect who rebuilt Windsor Castle, Jeffry Wyatville, might secretly have held it back). When the picture—which we later sold to the Queen amid a great fanfare of publicity—was delivered to our gallery we found a label on the reverse (not easily accessible as the plaster was so heavy). Having thought we had carried off a magnificent feat of independent detection, we saw the bland statement, in old handwriting, that this was a painting by Verrio of Charles II rescued from the old St. George's Hall. As now seemed to be the case with the newly arrived Gainsborough, the auction house had not heeded the most obvious clue available. From this label behind the Gainsborough, we were later to establish through Agnew's early records that they had bought it from a British seller named Mr. G. W. Grey in 1946—about whom, to date, we have found nothing. At least it suggested that the painting was highly unlikely to have been in America before that date.

One of the words most overused to describe attributing and judging a work of art is "instinct." There is certainly a place for it, but it is too often a mere catchall for the basic process of observation, releasing you from having to articulate your visual responses, which, in the case of an art dealer like myself, are in perpetual professional use. As I commit myself to paper I have tried hard to analyze the optical and mental process that takes place when the moment of physical (as opposed to digital or photographic) assessment comes. Apart from anything else, the purpose of this book is to try to communicate why I and others take the risks we do. There are many dealers (I would not necessarily describe them as the "sleuthers") who take no extreme risks, who at auction only buy paintings when they have clear, guaranteed attributions, which carry less hazard. If the price they end up paying is sufficiently advantageous, it allows them to make an honest profit. As dealers we live our professional lives with the confidence that we can do it better than the rank and file; but when it comes down to it, just as the pure academics are, we are fraily human. There is one characteristic, however, that I genuinely believe gives the professional buyer the edge: few things bring oxygen to the brain better than financial risk. Admittedly this normally applies *before* you have committed, and in the case of this painting it was *after*, but the principle remains the same providing you can muster honesty of response. For me there are four distinct phases.

Bendor lifted the picture facedown from the table and walked it over to the easel. The first look is often the most telling. Does it draw the eye? The answer in this case was yes: as Bendor and I stood before *Cornard Wood*, although it did not heave itself toward us like some great old master, its subtle composition and technique were both appealing and captivating. The next look then processes the content and the artistic devices used to impart it—the "clever" test, and this it also passed with merit. Although the figures were quite chunkily constructed, they were made so with certainty and clarity; the dash of light, the delicately observed tree trunks and dappled foliage had all the distinction and originality of a consummate artistic craftsman. Next comes a questioning of the evidence: Is what I am seeing genuine or overpainted? Is there damage that I have not noticed? Apart from a little flattening from a previous relining, and some allowable thinness in the more glazy areas of foliage of the upper branches, there was nothing to concern me here either—all par for the course. Finally there is the "further-away" assessment, which is vital for determining a picture's value and placing everything just processed into place. This normally involves reversing a few paces. I am usually so totally absorbed at this point, so rigidly focused on the object before me, that I have backed into people, furniture and, in one instance, a seventeenth-century canvas (in my restorer's studio) with considerable resultant damage.

Cornard Wood was everything I had hoped it would be. Once a yellow varnish was removed from the surface, I surmised, and the few localized passages of glaze repaired, it would revive into something compelling. Bendor was as pleased and relieved as I was, sharing in an enjoyment which can be likened to having played and landed a trophy fish, not least because under our halogen lamps the picture shone.

It took three months for the picture to be cleaned, relined and restored, and it returned with a confidence, poise and delicacy that could not fail to make one smile.

"You're too late," said the lady at the reception desk of Gainsborough's House. "The bulldozers have moved in and the building has started. And it's not called Cornard Wood anymore, either, but Chilton Homes—about 170 homes, to be exact."

I could barely believe what I was hearing.

"We all tried to stop it. Everyone tried, including that famous Mr. Attenborough man. I'm afraid you should have come last year. They're hard at it."

Although I knew there had been talk of developments around Cornard Wood, I had assumed it was one of those scary journalistic stories without foundation, reckless scaremongering to sell newspapers. On reflection, it was also because I could not realistically imagine a national treasure being allowed to be so savagely desecrated—the equivalent of placing a filling station on the site of Constable's *The Hay Wain* or a wind farm at Stonehenge. I turned to my eleven-year-old son, Oliver, who had accompanied me on this adventure, and he too looked bewildered.

"Let's go there anyway and have a look. At least we can see where it *was*," he said earnestly.

We had driven three hours from London, so I decided to make the most of Sudbury, and in a mood of some despondency took a rapid tour around Gainsborough's house. It had been ten years since I was last there and with recent restorations the old part of the house had become more historically atmospheric, stripped of its leaflet dispensers and rid of the intrusive sound of passing traffic. The portraits too, a number of which I had sold or acquired for the collection in the past twenty years, were now better lit and hung, able to smile back with appropriate pride for having been painted by the house's venerated former inhabitant. But they did little to exorcise images of ancient trees being bulldozed from the ground.

Great Cornard is a village on the southwest corner of Sudbury, and we set off there by car. We passed a shopping center and garage, turned right at a roundabout, then east up toward a track, at the top of which I could see a prominent chunk of woodland. A clear white sign stated that footpaths ended here, so we parked and covered the last few hundred meters on foot, mildy disturbed by the thought that we were now probably trespassing.

Reaching the wood involved crossing the edge of two further fields, and as we followed the hedge line I could not help thinking what a considerable walk from the center of Sudbury it was for a young lad—it had taken close to fifteen minutes to reach here by car. Apart from Abbas Hall, an ancient house behind trees visible from some distance back, we were remote and alone. I had been bracing myself for the pitiless sight of building works, at every turn expecting the trauma of broken earth and the discordant shapes and colors of machinery, construction trailers and company logos. To my growing surprise there were still none to be seen; it was a scorching June day and the only sights to behold were those of old Suffolk—a Prussian-blue sky, infinite greens, and scattered among high grasses flecks of red campion and Queen Anne's lace.

As we rounded the last hedge; Cornard Wood dramatically appeared before us, a blocklike citadel of trees at the top of the final stretch of slope. It was broader than I was expecting, and, unsure where to gain entry, I turned to find my bearings—to be met by an unfurling view across Great Cornard. It was blindingly spectacular and immediately suggested to me why Tom would have enjoyed perching himself away up here as a truant schoolboy. I looked down at the photograph of my picture, which Oliver was holding. If I could only spot Great Henny Church, I thought, then I might be able to orient myself to where he sat, but this was more challenging than I had reckoned. We squinted into the horizon for a whole half minute, and just as I was wondering whether we were in the right parish, let alone the right field, the solitary, sentinel shape of a church spire in the far middle distance came into focus.

"You go left and I'll go right," I instructed Oliver as we climbed the fence to enter the wood at what I calculated to be roughly the angle from which the steeple could be seen. "Let me know if you find water."

"But, Daddy, where are the bulldozers?" he asked, and alarmingly I could not help detecting concealed disappointment at having missed a drama.

"It appears they have yet to arrive," I said, feeling increasingly blessed that we had gotten there just in time. I was later to establish that the housing development was planned not for the wood but further down the slope toward Great Cornard, but not knowing that at the time, as I pushed through the outer branches, it was as though we had been miraculously granted a respite from time, a feeling that greatly increased as we entered the muffled silence of the wood. Surrounded by timeless growth, I was struck by the idea that everything was now as Gainsborough would have seen and felt it: the same coolness in contrast to the outside Gainsborough, the thicket of mare's tail and enchanter's nightshade around our feet, the stained-glass play of sunlight through broad leaves. I had been wandering only a few minutes, passing between the trunks and heading in no particular direction in search of anything that could be likened to a watery hollow with distant view, when Oliver called out.

"I can see it!" he bellowed from some distance away. "Quickly, come over here!"

He had run on a couple of hundred meters and I found him

next to a high bank, beyond some pheasant pens, triumphantly gesticulating to his discovery.

It was much broader than I had expected, and looked strikingly like the remains of an ancient, square-edged carp pond. On the far side it was bordered by a slope so densely covered with trees and nettles that it was impossible to detect its gradient or contour. To the right, through vegetation, lay the distant view of Great Henny we had been surveying earlier, but the undergrowth was so painfully thick it took a good fifteen minutes to negotiate our way around the pond, Oliver gingerly following, to an area at the water's edge that I felt equated to the position in which Tom had been sitting. While Oliver nursed his stings I cleared a place for us to sit on the damp, uneven ground and asked him to pass me the photograph that had remained clamped in his hand. I looked up through the canopy to the sky. Since we had entered the wood the sun had moved a few degrees to the west, and both the temperature and light had dropped. Although it was difficult to see clearly through the branches, I began to realize that the buildings and objects on the horizon and in the middle distance were now better delineated, as if the sun had conspired to cast them into relief.

Pushing aside some of the leaves in my immediate eyeline, I then found, to my sudden surprise, that the spire of Great Henny Church had transformed into an artistic baton, its express function, it now appeared, to orchestrate the composition. Looking outward from its tip to the foreground, I could now guess exactly where the marl diggers had been at work, where the orange-brown bank had been, where the path had once run and where the great, aging oak—now long gone—had been supplanted by a cluster of smaller trees, any one of which could achieve the same monumental distinction in centuries to come. The pond was much bigger than it appeared in the picture, but whether this was because it had been extended, or Tom had used artistic license, was unimportant: water completed the powerfully lyrical pattern of ground, tree, and sky.

I turned to Oliver and passed him back the image.

"Look, I think we've done it!" I said. "Can't you imagine how this would have filled Gainsborough's head—the water, the trees, the distant view?"

He looked at the photograph and then to the thicket of stems that now surrounded us.

"It's a good place to hide," he replied, and returned to rubbing his ankles with dock leaves to lessen the sting.

In the eighteenth century this was common land. Had I been Tom, I too would have sought a hideaway like this, a place of distant refuge remote enough to be an adventure, but within striking distance of home. Painters of the next few generations would seek inspiration—and risk their lives—by voyaging to such far-flung places as the Swiss Alps and the Middle East, and by scaling remote British mountains. For Gainsborough there was no need for such exotic exertions. By looking back across a woodland landscape toward his home, he had found his own version of the sublime.

We met Lindsay Stainton outside the staff entrance to the National Gallery. She was waiting with Diane Perkins, the new curator of Gainsborough's House, under whose directorship the museum has noticeably advanced in the past two years. Bendor stood next to me holding the picture, wrapped in brown paper, under his arm. Lindsay's reputation as a connoisseur is deeply established in the art world and she assisted John Hayes in the preparation of a number of his publications, so when some months earlier I had invited her to see the picture and she had proclaimed it an indisputable early work, on her suggestion we sought permission to see it next to *Cornard Wood* in the National Gallery. Another notable Gainsborough expert, Dr. Brian Allen from the Paul Mellon Centre in London, who had called around to my gallery earlier that month, had been unable to join us that morning, but we did have an eminent host, Dr. Susan Foister, head of British art at the National Gallery, as well as the past curator of a significant exhibition on early Gainsborough.

Susan had helpfully agreed to allow us to view the two pictures in the Gallery's conservation studio, which meant we could survey them at close quarters in optimum conditions. Having signed in at security and been greeted by her, we made our way along the high-ceilinged back corridors and then by lift to the upstairs studio, where the door was opened by Martin Wyld, acting director of the National Gallery and the much-admired head of conservation. This was not without irony, for a fact unknown to Martin until I told him was that his brother Andrew had been my underbidder.

I had forgotten how magnificent *Cornard Wood* was and was startled as I saw it there on the easel, morning light glinting off its surface from overhead windows. Free of its frame, it looked very different from the aloof landscape hanging some two feet above another painting on the Gallery's busy walls. I could appreciate its subtleties and incidents with newfound intimacy. Despite some fading and abrasions, it certainly deserved its reputation for greatness, its rustic observations working their magic on us as they had done to so many others over the past 250 years. While Martin went to prepare coffee Bendor carefully unwrapped our picture and walked forward to place it on an easel, a few paces to the right of *Cornard Wood*. He took care to fix it in place, and then stood back.

For myself and others there that day it was a moment of memorable poignancy. On the left was the great operatic masterpiece, one of the most admired productions of its day. On the right something altogether meeker and less contrived, but inextricably linked: a youthful precursor to the great things to come.

A sleeper had awoken as satisfactorily as it could do in my lifetime.

CHAPTER 3

The Norman Rockwell Hoax

Next time you go to an exhibition, spend some time looking at the people looking at the art. One of the most telling features of visitors to a gallery is that they will study the labels before they look at the pictures; in other words, facts are required before the visual process can kick in. More than that, however, the information on the label often dictates how the work of art is perceived, enjoyed and esteemed.

An extraordinary thing took place in the Norman Rockwell Museum in Stockbridge, Massachusetts, in the summer of 2006 and will remain forever in the annals of American art history. The incident is perhaps best expressed by Julie Brown, a museum guide of eighteen years' service, who arrived that fateful morning to discover her normally quiet museum, tranquilly set among woods on the outskirts of the town, to be overrun by press and television reporters. She wondered initially whether her employers were organizing some event, but quickly saw from the body language of the invaders that this was no academic symposium. A devotee of Agatha Christie, Julie was not intimidated by high drama in unexpected quarters. Nothing, however, had prepared her for the front-page international news story that had broken within the precincts of her own museum that morning, and which turned out to be every bit as sensational as one of the crime writer's greatest mysteries. Furthermore, this was non-fiction, in which she and her fellow staff had had an unwitting part to play. The felony was one of mind-blowing fakery. The victim was her beloved institution (among others). And the prime suspect was dead.

A little background is required. Julie and her fellow guides had been thrilled to receive on loan to the museum four years earlier Norman Rockwell's masterpiece *Breaking Home Ties*, a picture that had delighted the readership of the *Saturday Evening Post* when it had first been reproduced on its front cover, in September 1954. Voted the second most popular image in the *Post*'s history by its readers, the painting had played a prominent role in Rockwell's growing celebrity ever since, one of the iconic images that place him among America's best-loved painters and affirm him as his nation's greatest popular illustrator. It is easy to see why the readers, and indeed the guides, responded as they did: not only is the picture deftly constructed and painted, it is packed with pathos. A weather-beaten farmer, cigarette butt in mouth, waits with his bright-eyed son for the train that will take the boy off to college. There is the sense that by boarding the train and breaking his ties to home the youngster will leave his childhood forever. And there is a tension between the hope of youth and the acquiescence of age. This poignantly crafted domestic scene is cemented by the presence of the family collie, who rests its head adoringly on the boy's lap, completing the perfect allegory of socially evolving postwar America.

To me it is abundantly clear when a picture possesses what is sometimes crudely described as the "X factor"—such communicative power that even a passing barbarian would throw it a second look. "X factor" work can be any subject from the Massacre of the Innocents to a bunch of irises, any style from painfully detailed to broadly abstract; and when to these soul-touching images you add commercial scarcity, and the name of a great artist, even the hard-boiled self-made billionaires who never make a decision without a spreadsheet will allow emotion to rule. It is a time art journalists love, and art dealers wait for, when these often shadowy financial titans come out of hiding to snare these works, engaging in a trial by combat at auction, variously in person, via agents or by telephone. *Breaking Home Ties* could be described as just such a picture.

What had prompted the media invasion that day, however, was not a sale but something journalistically more spectacular. In a single stroke of revelation this emblem of mid-twentieth-century American art hanging on the Norman Rockwell Museum's walls, pored over by experts, esteemed by the public, famed for its history and sitting among other masterpieces by Rockwell, had been revealed as a fake. What was more, the unequivocal proof was obtained not by some process of scholarly analysis, or thanks to some unexpected breakthrough by scientific experts, but by something laughably simple. The real picture, from which it had been secretly copied, had reappeared.

My friend Rachel Kaminsky—whom I had met on my first trip to New York, when she was a director at Christie's, and who was now an independent dealer—first told me this story over the phone after reading it in the *New York Times* online. I responded with incredulity that so famous a picture, with so celebrated a history, could be harbored in the main museum devoted to the artist and yet turn out to be a copy. It sounded almost as farcical as being told that the Mona Lisa had been knocked off by a Montmartre street artist. Rachel, audibly amused as she read the story to me, suggested I should check it out. I agreed. From what she had read this sounded like the most revealing example of the type of art-world blindness that goes to the heart of many great discovery stories.

Every January there is a migration from London, Paris and Amsterdam of dealers in old masters to one or more of the major old-master sales in New York. As one of those who regularly make the journey I organized my 2008 visit so that I could spend a day or two extra on the Rockwell quest. A couple of years had passed since the big revelation, but a few e-mails and telephone calls suggested that those involved were disposed to talk, so I decided to spend no more than a day and night in New York, enough time to view in the flesh the pictures we had already studied online, and then take the early flight to Burlington Vermont, coincidentally to the same airport where seventeen years earlier I had gone to meet the late and eccentric collector Earle Newton.

There was only one sale to view, but it was a big one, with more than three hundred lots, and having spent three hours in the auction rooms with a halogen flashlight poring over the following day's offerings to establish condition and hunches, I called Bendor to discuss and arrange bids, and thus concluded the day's formal business.

Many New York dealers time exhibitions and parties to coincide with the sales, and later that evening I found myself on Madison Avenue at the gallery of Larry Steigrad and his wife Peggy Stone, their picture-filled emporium packed with figures from the art world. It was a welcome escape from the street, where the temperature had dropped to below freezing. They had come a long way since I had met them on my first trip to New York, now with annual shows, regular trips to exhibit at Maastricht and Palm Beach and a lavish art-world soirée each January. Throughout the evening I was able to swap notes with a raft of colleagues—Londoners such as Dave Dallas working with the old-master powerhouse Johnny Van Haeften, the nimble generalist Toby Campbell from Rafael Valls gallery and native New York light cavalry such as Peter Schweller and Robert Simon, both specialists in finding lost pictures. Milling in the throng that evening were restorers ready to ply their trade to the successful buyers, art historians who had lent their expertise to the cataloguers, art writers and journalists and even the auctioneer for the following day, George Gordon, who gave me honest insights into some of the pictures that were to fall beneath his gavel, including a curiously speculative Frans Hals I had decided to bid on (the one referred to in my introduction).

Just as I was leaving I noticed—to my surprise, given that Larry and Peggy are generally known for earlier works—a Rockwell on the wall. It was an illustration of army life, and a young art journalist whose name I never obtained was ardently explaining its merits to a compliant female listener. He was lecturing and gesticulating with no-nonsense Manhattan directness and this was too good an opportunity to miss, so I weighed in.

"You clearly rate Rockwell," I interjected, in retrospect a little heavy-handedly.

"Hard not to," he said, throwing me a mildly irritated look. "As I was just explaining, no artist could tell a story better. And for what it's worth," he added, turning back to his companion for emphasis, "he is the greatest illustrator in American art history. I have said so more than once."

I detected that as well as adding the finale to a thoughtfully crafted lecture, he had decided I was an Englishman in need of educating.

"But easily faked?" I provoked.

"Not really," he responded curtly. "He's too good, and all his works are recorded and reproduced. The books and catalogues on the artist are legion."

"Even *Breaking Home Ties?*" I inquired. He looked less sure of his ground now, and I could see he was working out whether he had bumped into a Rockwell scholar (though he needn't have worried).

"OK, that was an exception. But let me tell you something. There is stuff that does not add up there. I mean, frankly, how can you kid so many experts for so long? Then there was the discovery—can you really believe they found it the way they did? It is all too *Scooby-Doo.* Take it from me, there was funny business there."

"Funny business?" I replied with contrived innocence. "How fascinating. I shall have to ask the ex-owners when I see them on Friday."

Another momentary look of disquiet crossed his face as he wondered whether he had doubled his faux pas. When I explained that I was merely writing a book and had neither vested interest nor academic superiority, he remounted his platform.

"Mind yourself out there—it's not London. It's wild country!" He sought the eye of his companion and winked at her, and she compliantly smiled.

This little insight indicated that breaking through the perplexities was going to be more of a challenge than I had forecast. As I walked out of the gallery in the direction of the Waldorf-Astoria (the large Art Deco hotel on Park Avenue where I now always stay when in New York) I found myself musing on the possible outcomes of my meetings over the next two days. Perhaps there *was* a degree of funny business surrounding this, and if so, was a plodding English art dealer on a two-day trip to the country the right person to try to fathom it? I was also mindful that I was returning to the scene of the drama two years after it had happened, and this could prove both a drawback and a benefit: the protagonists' recollections may have faded; but equally, I consoled myself, recollections may be more revealing with the sedative of time. Any further reflections of an investigative kind abruptly ceased when the chill factor of Madison Avenue blasted me back to the mundane realization that my coat was back in the hotel, as was my wallet, and I had forty blocks to walk. It had also begun to snow.

I arrived in Burlington armed. In my bag, apart from my halogen flashlight, were two fat books on Norman Rockwell and his work. Now the truth is, you don't need to read much to appreciate why Rockwell is a towering giant of narrative or illustrative art. *Breaking Home Ties* is as good a picture as any to demonstrate this. There was nothing accidental about Rockwell's capacity to perform miracles of artistic entertainment. He staged the set, cast the actors, arranged the figures, chose the props and retained a balance between artistic ingenuity and the message for which he was being paid. It is no coincidence that the film director Steven Spielberg is a collector of his work, for both are masters at reaching a mass audience with a type of American storytelling that can enfold depth, humor and fantasy.

Rockwell took infinite pains with *Breaking Home Ties*. This period of his career saw him at the height of his artistic powers and gave rise to two other great works: *Shuffleton's Barber Shop* and *Marriage License*. The subject of *Breaking Home Ties* was particularly close to his heart as all three of his own sons had recently left home—the eldest had joined the air force and the others had gone away to college. Trying out different ideas with a camera, just as old masters used sketches and drawings, he experimented with a range of concepts, settings and models before latching on to the pictorial solution, at one stage nearly losing hope that he would ever find the right approach.

For the boy he first tried his son Tom, but soon he came to feel Tom didn't quite express the sentiment he was seeking. And then, by chance, in 1953, on a trip to the Philmont Scout Ranch in New Mexico, he plucked from obscurity one Robert Waldrop. He assiduously coached his new model to assume the appropriate facial expressions of expectancy and surprise, just as a film director might. Waldrop had the ideal combination of characterful youth and sturdiness; of particular note were his large feet and heavy hands, which Rockwell subtly used to accentuate his character's agricultural background. The model for the father came from closer to home in the person of a cousin of the family cook, a ravaged-looking Vermont farmer named Floyd Bentley. For the painting's setting he used photographs of the run-down train station in Thoreau, New Mexico, details of which he subtly enhanced in preparatory charcoal drawings. The fastidious image maker left nothing to chance.

From Burlington Airport, I drove for a couple of hours along sparsely traveled roads to Arlington, Vermont. It had started to snow again when I wound down the window to ask a local where the center of town was. He replied that I was in it. Given how little was going on, it was an easy mistake; there were remarkably few shops, a more than average number of churches and big gaps between houses.

When Rockwell arrived here in 1939, —already a celebrated front-cover illustrator for the *Saturday Evening Post* he would have been drawn not just by the clapboard simplicity and elegance of the town but by the dreamy allure of its surroundings— the postcard-white winters, the verdant springs and summers, an arcadia of trout rivers, dry-stone walls, pastures, mountains, and woods and the ecstatic hues of the Vermont fall. The core of the Arlington art group that would soon gather around their uncrowned king shared for the most part two attributes: they lived in handsome farmhouses, sometimes with considerable land (property was cheap), and they provided illustrations for the *Saturday Evening Post*. Until rival journalism, particularly television, took over, the *Post* was the most influential magazine in the country and, with a circulation of millions and a taste for commissioning high-quality art, offered the best vehicle a graphic artist could wish for. Rockwell was the Arlington Group's cohesive force and he set the tone, not just by dint of his towering stature but by virtue of what some have described as his honest good nature and regard for the community. Rockwell relied on the residents to pose for him—he eschewed professional models early in his career in favor of real people—and his knack for getting the best out of them added to the pleasure of a process that often ended with their faces achieving national recognition on the cover of the *Post*. With exposure bordering on celebrity the good folk of Arlington became passive role models framing the emotions of modern America.

Don Trachte, the picture's first owner, also worked for the *Post*, not as a painter but as a cartoonist. He had settled in Arlington with his wife, daughter and eldest son, Don, in 1949. Trachte's syndicated cartoon strip *Henry* was among the best known in America and centered on the exploits of a speechless child who in each adventure manages to overcome adversity by a combination of luck and guile. Although not a front-cover virtuoso like his neighbors and colleagues Mead Schaeffer (from whom he bought his house), Jack Atherton and Gene Pelham, Trachte, with his charismatic charm, tall stature and crisp Germanic features that reminded some of Ronald Reagan, cut a dashing figure in the community, and he quickly became a prominent part of the social scene, developing a strong friendship with Rockwell, for whom he sat as a model. Like most artists, particularly those living in close proximity, they would buy works from each other and in 1960, when the Southern Vermont Art Center held a retrospective Rockwell exhibition, Trachte made the substantial financial decision, with his wife, Elizabeth, to buy *Breaking Home Ties* from Rockwell for $900. Apart from spells at exhibitions, it remained with Trachte for almost all his life, a consecrated family artifact that every year became more valuable with his friend's ascending artistic stature.

Don Trachte died in 2005. His son Don, who was three when his parents established themselves in Arlington, arranged to meet me at the Arlington Inn, a snug skiing lodge set back from the road. This he had firmly recommended as the place to stay, though on driving through town I got the impression it was the *only* place. It had been quite challenging to contact Don Junior and it was only after the Rockwell Museum forwarded my requests that he e-mailed me to say he would be happy to talk. It was he who had negotiated the loan of his father's picture to the museum. Don and his siblings were thus the prime suspects. Could it really be that at no time had they had any inkling that they were duping the art world with a fake?

Don was certainly happy to meet once he knew my purpose and he provided faultless directions on how to find him; when I walked into the reception area at the Arlington Inn I found him standing expectantly before a log fire. He offered his hand with unguarded enthusiasm and once I had checked in suggested I ride with him to a diner farther along the main street, fittingly close to the defunct Green Mountain Diner, where the Arlington artists had met in the days of the town's creative distinction.

When we entered, two elderly locals with lined, winter-bitten faces and expressions of animated curiosity craned their heads to look over at us, requiring no more than a subject title to mutate into a saleable Rockwell painting. Looking around at the other patrons, I sensed that although the artists may have moved on, the neighborhood had not. Don led us to a window table and ushered me to a chair, and as he did so I tried to remind myself of his father's appearance. His dark eyes and faintly Teutonic features were reminiscent of a photograph I had seen of his father, but no more than that. He was clearly a good few inches shorter, and in his corduroy trousers, thick-knit blue sweater and loafers suggested more off-duty New York than bohemian Vermont. Don Junior now lived an hour's drive away in Burlington, close to where he had worked in military engineering, but, judging by the cheery greetings he received from the diner's proprietor, they had not forgotten him in Arlington. With native insight he guided me to the local speciality of chicken soup.

"I sat for Rockwell myself," Don reminisced over the strange-looking bowls of broth that appeared from the kitchen. "I was four years old and he asked me to sit on Santa Claus's knee with a girl of the same age. I behaved so badly that he had no choice but to paint our backs only. My father was furious, and I never got asked to pose again."

I began to notice disquiet in Don's manner. He wanted to tell me the whole story but he insisted it would take time. The journalists and film crews had come and gone and with them, in the ruthless stampede, had gone his side of the story. "I suppose in a way I have been perceived as the guilty party in all of this," he had told me the previous day when I rang to confirm my arrival time. After lunch he suggested we go directly to his father's studio, where he had arranged for his younger brother to meet me.

We drove for fifteen minutes past snow-filled gullies and fields with ponies in winter coats, and all the time he reminisced about the delights of his childhood, the neighbors they had enjoyed, his favorite haunts and the rivers he had swum in back in the late 1940s and 1950s. His recollections were occasionally tinged with darkness about present-day neglect, and as we

drove past Rockwell's sedate clapboard farmhouse and out-
buildings he excoriated the way the surroundings, in particular
an old school, had been allowed to degenerate.

I am sure I would have made a feeble police inspector for the
simple reason that I empathize too much with my suspects. I
found myself liking Don, who struck me as one of those sensitive, quiet Americans with an earnest desire to live, prosper and,
where possible, do the right thing. Perhaps he *had* just unwittingly found himself at the center of one of the most extraordinary national art stories of the decade and was seeking to make
sense of his part in it? Or was I being well and truly duped, as the
art world had been for so many years?

Deducing motive is to my mind central to success. The
ultimate parable illustrating this for me was a trip I had
taken with my wife and seven-year-old son to the souk in Marrakech in search of an old rug for our London house. The word
went around the market that we were there to buy something of
significance, and with telepathic speed six or more competing
rug dealers fell upon us, tugging us in separate directions like a
pack of hyenas and forcing us down a side alley. It was in danger
of turning nasty when we were rescued by a very tall, noble-
looking Berber dressed in a traditional caftan and fez, who dispersed the mob with sharp words, wielding a wooden staff. He
spoke perfect English and took us to the refuge of his house,
gave us tea and profusely apologized for the reprehensible
behavior of his fellow citizens. Just as my optimism in human-
ity was reviving, and we were considering returning to the hotel,
he told us there was something we needed to see. From a corner

of the room behind a curtain he produced fifty rugs and would not let us leave till we had bought one from *him*.

The need to read body language and register motive is certainly elemental to my business, particularly with sellers. It involves assimilating all the available evidence and signals combined with courteous prodding. Marrakech notwithstanding, it is something I am generally good at. I bolstered myself now with the thought that I could resort to the same survivalism with Don.

"Up there is where it all took place," Don declared five minutes later, turning off the main drag. We ascended a steep, pine-filled slope that was clearly leading us to a vantage point of sorts at the head of the valley. It felt remote, as if we were pushing up and away from the basin of civilization.

"My father's studio—the place where it all happened," he announced again portentously.

We had drawn up in front of what must once have been a modest, cube-shaped Vermont farmhouse that had subsequently hybridized into a seventies confection. A substantial concrete platform divided by water channels thrust out on one side, and wooden and glass structures on the others. The Vermont winters had done their work too, and some of the paint beneath the eaves and windows was peeling and stained. This mild sense of dereliction also pervaded the surrounding gardens. Pushing through the snow like the archaeological remains of an ancient settlement were crumbling stone walls, bridges and rockeries. Don guided me around to the back door.

"We kind of left it as it was when he died a few years back, and nothing has been done to patch it up," he said, unlocking the door, his voice filling with sentiment as he led me into the hallway. "The more I discover my father, the more I am amazed by him. He poured his own cement and basically built everything around us with his bare hands."

There was an odor of dampness, only adding to the aura of what was beginning to feel like a shrine. On the walls were constant reminders of his father's life and acquaintances—photographs of fellow artists, a framed letter from an American president, and numerous paintings and drawings by a variety of hands but mostly by neighbors and contemporaries.

"I really am astonished by what he did," Don reflected as he began to walk me around the house. "He crossed so many areas of creativity and just look at these paintings . . ." Don had taken me into a side room filled with crates of Wild West scenes, portraits and landscapes painted in soft, brushy colors testifying to his father's feverish desire to find a language in paint, although, as he pulled them out one by one, try as I might I was unable to imagine them causing a stampede in a New York art show. Trachte's first calling was clearly a pencil rather than a brush.

We moved to the huge studio room and Don sat down on a worn leather sofa, apologizing for the condition of the upholstery as he offered me the armchair opposite. Over his head, through the immense studio windows I could see trees and a valley, at the end of which, almost as a landscaped focal point, were the sloping fields of Norman Rockwell's farm. The room was huge, natural light flooding through the large windows as brightly as if we had been sitting in a cow field. A balcony of twisting birch branches ran along the upper part of one wall, and paintings and personal mementos covered the rest of the room's available wall space.

"That will be Dave," Don said brightly as a car drew up.

Moments later a man in a baseball hat, leather-trimmed shirt and Timberland boots, a good degree taller than his elder brother, entered the room. His steady delivery, weather-beaten face and powerful handshake completed the contrast. Don had earlier explained to me that Dave had not left the valley like his sister and two brothers but had opted out of formal education, married a local girl and set up a business repairing cars farther down the road.

Dave took a seat next to Don and as they both looked at me I got the sense of powerful unity, a collaborative bond. I was later to discover that the mountain man rather than his urbane elder brother was the definer of the family's destiny.

"So how did it all begin?" I asked. As I got out my notepad and pencil and the brothers exchanged glances to see who would go first I started to feel even more like a novice investigator embarking on his first case. Watch their body language, I thought. Imagine they have just turned up at the gallery with a Van Dyck wrapped in refuse sacks, with the story that they inherited it from an aristocratic ancestor.

"I can remember my father first arriving with the picture in 1960," Don began. "He unloaded it from his Volkswagen bus and then hung it on our living-room wall in the most prominent place over the grand piano. It was a major event, and there was a feeling that this was now our prize possession." He thought for a moment and then added, "It was a great picture, one of those images you responded to as a kid—your eyes go straight to the farmer and then bounce off to the boy. We should have kept that in mind."

He looked over to Dave, who smiled complicitly.

"We were all rather awestruck at having it in the house,"

Don continued. "There were lots of parties, smoking and drinking in the room, and frankly why it didn't get damaged by the baseball we used to surreptitiously play with in there, I don't know. During the early sixties the price of Rockwell's work was escalating and amazingly within six years Dad was able to turn down an offer for $35,000—not bad for an investment of $900. Rockwell was aware of the offer and wrote to Dad to say that he must be crazy for turning it down, but that he loved his loyalty for doing so!"

Don went on to explain how things then started to go wrong between their parents, and I found myself being led behind the doors of a family who, had it not been for this picture, would never have had the need to divulge so much to a stranger. The breakdown in the relationship, he said, culminated in their decision to divorce. It was a tough and prolonged negotiation not least because the Rockwell, together with seven other pictures, ranked among the main assets for discussion, and it took three years to resolve the issue. Its ending was not just a relief to their father—who had been living on his own during this time—but also to the children. The outcome also appeared fair: the pictures would be formally made over to the children, but during his lifetime their father was allowed to live with and enjoy the Rockwell and two of the others: a George Hughes and a Claire Weinz flower piece. Their mother was given similar custodial rights over the remaining five pictures.

Don spoke like someone who wished to inform rather than conceal, and I felt my guard lowering. He explained how his father bought and moved into the house in which we were sitting, then just a small Vermont home, which over time he expanded while their mother remained in the family home, a short drive down the tree-filled slope. This allowed the children, by then adults, to make regular visits to both parents.

"On one such visit to my father I remember being aware of some mildly out-of-keeping, mass-produced wood paneling that he had installed along one wall of the studio," Don added, and the triviality of this recollection gave me the impression he was about to announce something. "It incorporated a deep-shelved bookcase filled with ornaments. As he was perpetually adding to the house it didn't strike me as significant."

He then returned to chronicling family history: before I could get to the crime scene, he would finish his story.

By the 1980s, he explained, Arlington's artistic commune had all but vanished—Rockwell had moved to Stockbridge in 1953 in order to be closer to his wife, Mary, who was undergoing therapy for depression at the nearby Austen Riggs Center, and most of the original *Saturday Evening Post* crowd had retired, died or moved on, but his father's creative fervor was apparently undimmed, and he worked continuously on both his house and his art, laboring by day and painting and drawing at night. Although increasingly reclusive, he had fallen for and married a local girl named Liz Ayres, a union that proved to be both sustaining and happy until she fell ill in the early 1990s. Nursing her, Don told me, had exhausted his father and, too frail to continue in the house, he went into assisted living, leaving the house and its contents behind.

For the children this raised the obvious practical question of what to do with the Rockwell. Conscious that a national treasure hung inside—a painting which after all belonged to the four of them—after family discussions, and with his father's compliance, Don Junior approached the nearby Rockwell Museum.

This seemed both logical and practical: a perfect temporary home for so valuable a work of art where, as a loan, it could at the very least be enjoyed by the public.

Aware that I needed to approach this story from two directions, the previous day, I had driven along icy roads in my rental car from the airport to the remote museum on the outskirts of Stockbridge, in the Berkshire Mountains. From a distance it exuded more the air of an imposing private residence than a museum. I had been told by the curator to find lunch before I arrived because it was too far from the center of town to pop out for a bite. It may have been the weather or the time of year, but there were no other visitors in the museum's main gallery when I entered, which offered me the opportunity to take my first plunge into Rockwell's world in lavish solitude.

As I stood in the middle of the room, my eye ranging across its walls, I absorbed each of the twenty or so images in turn. I now saw where *Breaking Home Ties* had fit in and belonged. The ebullient characters, playful, industrious, introspective and dynamic, expressed a society on the move, so different from the utilitarianism of a war-weary Britain. These twentieth-century allegories were brilliant reflections of aspirational young America: no wonder, I thought to myself, susceptible collectors are so powerfully drawn, spilling blood to secure the best.

"I'm glad you found us. If you want peace, quiet and safety, then Stockbridge is the place you want to be." Linda Szekely Pero, the curator of the Norman Rockwell Collection, had emerged from the downstairs offices and had slightly surprised me in my musings. An impressively comprehensive scholar on the subject of her artist, Linda had grown up in New York and attended what she described as a progressive liberal arts college in Vermont before joining the museum. We had had a number of telephone discussions during which it had become clear to me that she was an important *dramatis persona* in the picture's story.

Linda led me down to the museum's airy basement library and introduced me to the assistant director, Stephanie Plunkett. It was Linda who had been most intimately involved in the Trachtes' loan, and although she had been elswhere when *Breaking Home Ties* arrived, in 2002, she had been closely concerned with its time at the museum. The immediate question I wanted to ask was whether the painting had ever struck her as in any way strange or different—a question that was inherently provocative given what it subsequently turned out to be. As we got talking I found her to be noticeably open. And yes, she did have concerns, she told me, but ones which she had forced herself to lay to rest.

"I felt it somehow lacked something when I first saw it," she recalled. "I put it down to the strip lighting in the room and it also had a badly termite-eaten frame."

As an art dealer I have learned that although lighting is crucial to a painting's presence, its surround can be pivotal too. Many paintings, particularly old masters, lack their original frames and require new ones. These can be commissioned from workshops, or old ones can be bought from specialist dealers or at auction and then cut down or adapted to fit. (We have our own in-house craftsman whose job is specifically to do this.) Framing is a surprisingly challenging science, and if the color, design or proportions are wrong, much as with the clothes you choose to wear, a glamorous picture can be reduced to a dowdy frump. Linda's response—a questioning of the painting followed by its acquittal—was fascinatingly revealing.

The first person to voice misgivings, and then explain them away, had actually been the museum's former director, David H. Wood. Linda took me to the other end of the library to play me an old tape recording from the early 1980s. The library's archives of items relating to Rockwell were understandably comprehensive, down to musings and interviews that could be useful. So we listened to the formal tones, reminiscent of an early radio broadcast, of Wood's voice from the grave. A man who did not mince words, he recalled seeing the picture in the late seventies, when it was on exhibition at the Bennington Museum in Vermont. Although he thought it was "awful," crucially he did not challenge its authenticity, preferring instead to ponder whether it was a preparatory rather than a final work. He reported discussing this with Rockwell's son Jarvis, who then introduced a concept that a number of doubting Thomases satisfied themselves with thereafter: he concluded that at some point it had been overcleaned, which had removed glazes, and that what could now be seen was underpainting rather than the finished product. This view was latched onto by a visitor to the museum who had some authority on the matter, a summer student of Rockwell's in the late 1940s named Don Spaulding. When he saw *Breaking Home Ties* soon after its arrival at the museum, in 2002 he told Linda that he had watched Rockwell working on the painting. " 'You should have seen it, it glowed,' " she recalled his saying, "and it broke his heart to encounter it as it looked then."

Linda decided to pursue another line of inquiry. By way of explanation she advanced the tape to a second recording, from around the same date. This one was an interview with Louis Lamone, who had been an assistant to Rockwell after his move from Arlington to Stockbridge in 1953. Lamone had perfect recall of the picture being painted, and with compelling exactitude recollected that Rockwell had had to add another inch on one side because the *Post*'s printers had told him it did not fit their format; it was therefore taken off its stretcher and the necessary extension was added. Surely, Linda had thought to herself, if I examine the picture out of its frame I should be able to detect this in some way? She duly did so, when it was hanging in the racks in temporary storage, but despite a thorough investigation she was unable to find any sign of the addition. "I thought this would be the perfect way to verify it," she told me, "but tiresomely it revealed nothing."

Next Linda aired some of her concerns with Don. They agreed to send the painting to the Williamstown Art Conservation Center in Massachusetts, regional experts in restoration who had twenty years' experience with Rockwell's paintings. They assiduously analyzed the painting, and although they could find no evidence that it had been extended, they did conclude that it was entirely consistent with Rockwell's technique. They also cleaned it, which helped the colors function better.

There was one man, however, who would not be assuaged. As an artist, more specifically a portrait painter, John Howard Sanden was a devotee of Rockwell and, of all the museums he had visited, the Norman Rockwell Museum was his favorite. He loved its elegant design but also its exclusive focus, not least (I suspect) because his own work, with its clean-shaven, traditional subjects technically owes something to Rockwell's style for expressing the myth of modern America. His sitters appear to have a good feeling about themselves, and, although they are untesting as works of contemporary art, he composes the sort of family portraits that comfortably slip into the middle-class interior in a way that will never scare pets or grandchildren. Rated by some as among the ten most successful portraitists in America, Sanden, with his two studios, in Connecticut and New York City, and his smoothly professional presentation skills, had become a figure who could not easily be overlooked. In the late 1950s and the 1960s he had had the intriguing job of art director for the preacher Billy Graham, and when he first saw *Breaking Home Ties* hanging at the museum he responded with a combination of artistic indignation and evangelical zeal.

"He returned a number of times," Linda recalled, "and frankly scared the staff, who had to ask him to stand back from the picture because of his demonstrative hand gestures."

A master of website communication, Sanden would not be silenced. "What was going on here?" he asks in a posting which as of this writing can still be found. "What was a world class museum doing showing an inferior replica?" In the same posting he claims to have written seven letters to the museum to state his case without receiving a considered reply.

Linda and her fellow staff were irked by Sanden's protestations but nonetheless decided to accept the picture for what they thought it was—a Rockwell that had been bought by Don Trachte from the artist, but that had been damaged in some way, quite possibly, Linda surmised, when it was exhibited in Russia and Egypt in the mid-1960s after the canvas had been rolled up—an old-fashioned technique for conveniently sending works long distances that would give today's conservators coronaries. The different climatic conditions it had suffered while traveling might also, she considered, have detrimentally affected its appearance, so that when it returned it would have required considerable restoration and conservation.

Don had come to hear of Sanden's dissatisfaction and was now regularly reading his website. Having established the background, Don was moving the story forward. His pace had changed and it almost felt as if events were unfurling in real time. I had the benefit of being able to match two perspectives: that of the museum, rattled but resolved to sedately continue in their affirmation of the work's authenticity; and that of the owners, bewildered and frustrated, now wondering whether lending the painting had been a good idea at all.

The children had decided that they wanted to explore selling the painting. It had been insured for $3.5 million but in the ascending market was now likely to make considerably more: every few months the major newspapers had been reporting record-breaking prices for twentieth-century masters, and the desire to ride this was pressing on them. But, in addition to Sanden's regular transmissions, other things were now beginning to trouble the family—strange, seemingly isolated circumstances that began to coalesce with sinister implications.

In 2004, the Illustration House, New York's leading commercial gallery and auction house devoted to illustrative art, asked to borrow another picture from the family collection, *Head Tied*, a scene in a printroom by Mead Schaeffer. But when Don sent them a photograph they politely declined on the basis that there appeared to be discrepancies between the Trachtes' picture and the published illustration. "This caused us considerable concern at the time," Don recalled, "but we were all so busy we did not get too hung up." The disquiet, temporarily buried, would return.

Don Trachte Sr. died in 2005, two weeks before his ninetieth birthday, and in July of that year his children held a small service of remembrance at a local church. They repaired to their father's house for a family gathering, during which one of them, by chance, found in a closet a painting by George Hughes called *Green Herons*. That would not have been strange in itself, except that it was an *exact* replica of another Hughes picture that was hanging nearby on the wall. So close were they in appearance that, for the children at least, it was impossible to tell them apart.

The confluence of Sanden's website campaign, the rejection of Schaeffer, and the Hughes in the closet was now too much to ignore. The noose tightened when later that year Don went to New York to Illustration House—not, as it happened, for any other reason than to discuss the identification of some cartoons that had belonged to his father.

"The gallery's founder, Walt Reed, seemed a bit nervous and distracted," Don explained. "Then his son Roger, the gallery's president, joined him, and they said they would like to talk to me. I got the impression they had something of great importance to relate. As it turns out, they did. 'Somewhere, sometime, something has happened to *Breaking Home Ties*,' Walt told me solemnly. In retrospect I now realize they were trying to let me down gently." As both father and son were published experts on the subject of American illustration, this euphemistic detraction was as good as a fatal pronouncement.

"I came home depressed and told the others, 'Folks, I think

we are stuck,'" Don said. "What made matters worse was that I had a call from Peter Rathbone, head of modern American art at Sotheby's, telling me that this would be a great time to sell and it could be slated for a spring auction. I found myself in a terrible dilemma and suggested to Peter that perhaps we should authenticate it first. 'Why would we question it?' he asked. 'It's been in your family all the time.'"

Don felt he was stuck. If he told Peter Rathbone everything he now knew it would scupper an auction sale. This was a hugely valuable family asset, of apparently impeccable provenance and to the right collector—who could surely make up his own mind—the ultimate acquisition. And it was, after all, hanging on the Rockwell Museum's walls: What greater imprimatur could there be than that?

Dave now entered the conversation to explain how he had taken it upon himself to make his own investigations. Dave was a pragmatist used to addressing and solving mechanical problems; he talked with the same precision as Don but with the irony of a younger brother now telling the story *his* way. To me, the third of four siblings myself, it rang true and took me closer to the conclusion that they were hapless victims of their father's contrivance.

Dave's response embodied a touch of his father's do-it-yourself approach. Something did not add up; in order to solve the mystery he needed to understand what piece had broken down and then fix it. He was better placed than his brother to do so. Unlike Don, who was working in Burlington, Dave was just down the road and could regularly visit the lonely, now unoccupied, house to collect his thoughts and test theories. He had studied the picture and compared it with a tear-sheet of the cover of the *Saturday Evening Post* and was under no illusion that they did not *appear* different. From that starting point there had therefore to be an explanation. He began to search for clues, and now, with a more informed sense of what to look for, he took each room in turn, poring over his father's mostly untouched possessions, deliberating on the significance of everything he found.

His methodical application soon bore results. Buried among copious other photographs, he found two old photographs of *Breaking Home Ties*. At first he thought them identical, but as he carefully studied them it began to become apparent to him that they differed minutely. His eye going from one to the other, he worked out that this was no trick of light or focus: they were two different pictures, the one they owned and another, fractionally closer in appearance to the illustration that had appeared in the *Post*. Dave rose from his chair and handed the two photographs to me as if they were courtroom exhibits. Despite their slightly bleached appearance I could see how the boy's expression differed, but the photographs were not clear enough for me to be sure exactly how. For Dave, however, this had been the proof he required, and he then applied himself to the hunt with even greater zeal.

Digging further into his father's papers, he had managed to locate the numbered negatives for the roll of film and with it a startling revelation: the photo of their Rockwell was taken *before* the other—thus going some way toward establishing that theirs could not be the same picture with repairs, damage or repainting. Now animated by his progress, Dave was each night on the telephone discussing every new thought and revelation with Don, while continuing his solitary visits to root around the house. The next advance he was able to report was that he had found in a storeroom a large roll of canvas that would fit their picture, together with an empty plywood packing case of similar dimensions. And yet the sons/brothers agreed that so far as they could remember, their father never painted pictures on this scale.

Don and Dave decided to keep these discoveries to themselves and not tell Linda Szekely Pero at the museum but instead to calmly develop a hypothesis on their own. Three options remained in play, which they juggled in regular phone calls at night: that there were no differences between the two pictures and their eyes were playing tricks on them; that the picture had been damaged in Russia or Egypt when it was on exhibition, or accidentally by their father at a later date; or, as now appeared increasingly plausible, that their father had painted a replica. The discovery of the numbered negatives seemed to rule out damage, but as it was the most attractive option, in May Don arranged for the picture to go back to the conservators in Williamstown with the instruction that they should carefully examine and analyze the boy's face to see if there were any signs of alterations or repairs. The somber answer came back that there were none.

Don, extremely busy at work in Burlington on a project to supply a large radar system to the military, was frustrated not to be able to collaborate in person with Dave in his forensic investigations of the family home, but he did agree to go there for a weekend in mid-March. Dave, in the meantime, kept searching behind mirrors and furniture and in every other possible hideaway until he ran out of places to look. On the Thursday before they were due to meet, having found nothing further of significance, Dave decided to turn his attention to the fabric of the house itself, and in particular the walls. There was frankly nowhere else left to go. He started in the studio room. Examining the paneling that had been erected by his father in the 1970s with a mechanic's methodology, Dave tapped, pushed and squeezed anything that might not be fixed, until he discovered a noticeably loose plank. He carefully levered it back to open a crevice just wide enough to peer into with a flashlight. Its beam fell on a partitioned area about ten inches deep, in which, to his inordinate thrill, he could just make out the edges of two hanging canvases—one big, the other small.

He stopped what he was doing and rang his brother.

"I think I've found something," he said, guarded yet jubilant, "but I'm not going any further till you come down here!"

It was the Thursday before St. Patrick's Day, Dave recalled, and despite the demands of work Don decided to leave early, at noon. Sitting across from me, both brothers were now wreathed in smiles and almost talking in unison as they recounted how Don arrived with a bag of demolition tools, only to be told by Dave that he would not need them. Their father was too good a craftsman for that; all they would require were their hands and a little brainpower. Dave had largely figured out how the jigsaw-like apparatus held together, and after removing ornaments and decorative wooden boxes the brothers dismantled the shelves one by one. The bottom one had a return that extended around the paneling to its right, and on removing it they revealed runners that were clearly designed to allow something to be drawn back. It could only be the adjoining panel wall. When they pushed the section, which measured eight feet by four feet, it gave way with ease. Almost paralyzed with astonishment, like Howard Carter discovering the tomb of Tutankhamen, they saw, in previously darkened solitude, five oil paintings—the very same pictures they thought had been distributed in the divorce settlement. In an instant they realized what had happened. In the early seventies, when their mother had moved out, but before concluding the divorce negotiations, their father must have made copies and secretly retained the originals. The authentic works, with the exception of the Hughes that they had already found (though not then realizing its significance), were the paintings they were now gazing at.

There was no sign of the Rockwell. But they had only opened the outer tomb. The ultimate discovery required sliding back the adjoining panel, which, as it turned out, was exactly behind the spot where *Breaking Home Ties* had hung before it went on loan. Rarely does an artistic discovery come with gratifyingly instantly as it did to the two brothers at that moment. In the art world, tangible revelation normally follows a painfully uncertain process of restoration as a picture's true form and identity is gradually uncovered. Not so here. With a slide of the wall a year of uncertainty was put to rest, every clue explained, the spectral shadow that had haunted the siblings' peace of mind roundly exorcised. The Rockwell hung before them, together with another picture from the cache, its surface glowing almost as pristinely as if it had just left the artist's studio,—and, as Don added with a note of triumph, the canvas conspicuously included a tacking edge where it had been extended for the printers. There could be no better signature of genuineness than that.

Having enjoyed the tumultuous elation of their discovery, Don now turned his mind to how to break the story to the Rockwell Museum. It would have to be handled carefully. There was bound to be an element of incredulity, initially at least, and if they were not properly mindful this could lead to allegations of deception and obfuscation on their part, particularly as they had been in possession, prior to the discovery, of strong circumstantial evidence that the picture might be a fake. Although the quest had ended, their adventure with the art world was just beginning.

Stephanie Plunkett, the assistant director of the museum, arrived at work on Monday morning to find a message on her answering machine. It was from Don and had been left the previous day. He sounded uptight but gave no details as to why he had called and simply said, "We are coming to see you." Stephanie and Linda met the brothers later that day and led them to a private office where they could talk confidentially. Don began by saying, "We've got some good news and some bad news." Both women remember how, after this tantalizing introduction, they listened to Don's measured account of the various stages of the family's growing concerns. They wondered when and where this story might lead. After twenty minutes Don reached the finale: the painting hanging on their walls, he concluded, was a copy by his father.

Linda recalls a sense of relief surfacing through her shock at the disturbing disclosure. At least, she thought, that explains the doubts. Stephanie hotfooted it off to report what had happened to the museum's director, Laurie Norton Moffat, and plans were immediately put in place for a group from the museum to visit the house. The director and Stephanie, together with a conservator, Sandra Webber, their PR director, Kim Rawson, and two art handlers set off the next day and returned to the Trachte house later that week with the now discredited *Breaking Home Ties* to make a side-by-side physical comparison. There could be no doubt: this was the real thing.

Over the next few weeks Don and Dave would have to break this news hundreds of times, including to their mother, who at eighty-nine had lost none of her skepticism about her ex-husband, despite the passage of time and her subsequent remarriage. Sitting in her chair at the farmhouse down in the valley, surrounded—until then unwittingly—by her husband's fakes, she listened intently and silently to the story with her hand on her mouth till the end. "It doesn't surprise me," she said acidly.

The museum had some explaining to do, not least to John Howard Sanden. To this day he defines himself as the only one to have remained "firm in the contention that the painting on exhibit for nearly three years was a fake." The PR mechanism was effective and swift: Sanden and his wife were invited to lunch with the museum's director and received what he described as a "very gracious and sincere apology," which he accepted with "understanding and sympathy." The museum's staff, having carefully considered how to handle what could be deemed a severe embarrassment in the museum world, responded with dexterity: they held a comprehensive exhibition around the whole episode, curated by Stephanie, putting both pictures and telling the story of Don Trachte Senior and the Arlington art group.

Those who visited the exhibition, which was assembled quickly and opened two weeks after the discovery, were able to see the two pictures side by side, and so could make up their own mind as to whether they would have fallen for the fake. Although I did not have the benefit of seeing the fake with the original, Don and Dave gave me the opportunity to examine their father's copy, which they held back till the end of our conversation. Although I have bought many copies of originals, only once (as far as I know) have I unwittingly bought what could be described as a deliberate fake of a known artist. A minor London auction house had offered a twelve-inch-high self-portrait by the famous British faker Tom Keating, best known for his counterfeits of valuable works by the nineteenth-century watercolorist Samuel Palmer. I bought it in the belief that it would be a good painting to have in stock for the well-fed collector who wanted a witty aside to add to his collection. It was only when I picked it up from the auction house and examined the reverse of the canvas, then looked up the manufacturer's stamp, that I realized it was painted *after* Tom Keating's death: I had bought a fake of the faker. What intrigued me about *Breaking Home Ties* was the scale and ambition of the sham. The picture was forty-four inches square and full of technically demanding shapes, recessions and tones, added to which was the fact that the work of Rockwell was as familiar to the American public as any twentieth-century artist's could be. Don Trachte had chosen a tough act.

Don and Dave hauled the painting out of a back room and unwrapped it for me in the large studio. Although it was then late afternoon and the shadows were lengthening, the daylight lingered sufficiently to illuminate its surface. I was fascinated by the prospect of putting myself to the test. They propped the canvas against the sofa, facing the main window, and I knelt before it.

At first glance it looked plausible. The paint had the luster and finish I remembered from other Rockwells at the museum. No wonder it had come back from the conservators with a clean bill of health, I thought. As a close friend and model, Trachte must have observed the master down to the compounds he used and the way he applied his brush, a privilege open to very few fakers.

But there is something a conservator or restorer cannot see, and this I suppose is where connoisseurship sometimes overtakes science. I had the grossly unfair benefit of hindsight, but the longer I looked, the more I noticed shortfalls. The first was a certain shallowness. Despite the correctness of the pigments and the way they shone, the shapes and recessions appeared too certain, lacking the sense of development you would expect from an artist originating a work from drawings, photographs, observation and his own memory. I stood up, took a few paces back and now noticed how the farmer's head lacked volume and that his lips failed to quite follow the contours of his jaw. Then I registered faintly saggy areas of description in the bodywork of the car and, now that my eye was tuned, in the surrounding architecture too.

Most noticeable of all, however, was the emotional focal point of the picture—the boy's face. This was where Trachte had most noticeably given himself away. As humans we have highly sensitive receptors for registering the nuance of expression: it is a science perfected since the cradle. To precisely replicate a painted expression, even for an artist copying his own work, is a near impossibility. Comparing the boy's expression with the one on the tear-sheet cover Don had passed me, I now registered two different faces.

On November 29 the Trachte children and their partners were ushered into a private room next to the auction gallery on the eighth floor of Sotheby's imposing New York headquarters on York Avenue. The auction house had organized the ultimate showcase for the sale of so great a trophy: a catalogue dedicated solely to the picture, replete with illustrations, portrait photographs, scholarly contributions and a full account of its history had been distributed to collectors worldwide; the Sotheby's publicity machine had been carpet-bombing the press with the story of the painting's dramatic resurgence, and now its availability to the highest bidder; favored or likely clients had been given the opportunity to see it before the view days. The family had agreed to a pre-sale estimate of $4–6 million, well in excess of their insurance valuation, but even that could prove conservative in the prevailing market conditions. The previous auction record for a Rockwell was $9.2 million, for *Homecoming Marine*, sold at Sotheby's in May of that year, and there were those who believed this record could be broken.

The Trachte clan gathered around a video screen in a side room near the auction and were able to watch the family's financial destiny unfold in virtual reality as their father's beloved painting appeared on the rostrum and the bidding began. The auctioneer, Dara Mitchell, opened at just below the lower estimate and the Trachtes sat adhered to their chairs as the bidding sedately climbed. When it had reached $10 million they realized the roof had been lifted and anything was now possible. They kept on willing the bids to increase, and their exhortations worked. *Breaking Home Ties* exceeded all records for the artist by making just over $15 million—a price for the artist that as I write has yet to be broken. Although at the time there was some speculation that Steven Spielberg was in the running, the buyer to this day remains anonymous.

Don suggested we go for dinner at a special place he knew, a restaurant high in the mountains over Arlington. There, he said, we would be joined by his partner, Michelle, whom he had described more than once as an important sounding board and companion during the final months of their ordeal. As we sat in the bar awaiting her, a local band was setting up behind us, and the proprietor's six- or seven-year-old daughter, perched on the carpet, counted out a bowl full of dimes, sprightly calling out her tally as she approached 100.

I chose not to ask Don what he and his three siblings had done with their proceeds of the sale—it felt too crass (although I gather Dave did go out and buy a new tractor)—but I did want to know what he thought his father had been up to, and why he had not told them his secret before he died. It seemed obvious that Don Senior had embarked on the fraud in the early 1970s, when the marriage settlement was being discussed. The fact that after three years' negotiation he ended up as the lifetime keeper of the main picture was not something he could have forecast. Once he was committed to his plan, particularly after friends, family and visitors had become familiar with the fakes, he perhaps felt he could not risk exposing any of them as not being the real thing. Besides, who knows, maybe privately he relished the fact that his artistry could be every bit as good as his more famous contemporary, for chippiness is often one of the motives that drive a faker.

"As we grew up," Don recalled, "he became increasingly reclusive. His work was off-limits to us and we became distanced from him as time went on. Every time we speak about him now we try to work out what he was up to. And then there were the clues—not just the ones we found before, but also afterwards."

Don produced a folded piece of yellow paper that he had found among the documents in his father's safe after his death. It was a diagram consisting of seven rectangular shapes correlating exactly to the size and position of each picture hidden behind the paneling. There were no words or explanations, just this simple maplike drawing. When he first went through his father's possessions Don had entirely overlooked it, but since the discovery its relevance had hit him. The fact that his father had locked the document in a safe he regarded as highly significant.

"So it seems he was trying to lead us to something," Don said.

"But only after his death," I probed.

"That's true—though we got there in the end."

"What is your considered view as to why he did it?"

"I have sometimes thought that perhaps he painted the pictures for security, in case they were stolen. The thieves would then end up with worthless copies," Don answered.

"But it wouldn't have prevented him from telling you," I pointed out gently.

"Yes, but perhaps he just went to sleep at the wheel. He

crossed over into another time zone. It was just something he forgot to tell us."

Michelle arrived and we went into the restaurant. A sophisticated, elegant woman in her fifties who had trained in psychology, she had been Don's partner for four years and from what he had told me, and the proud way he presented her, was a pivotally supportive element in his life.

We placed our orders and with Don's guidance I chose a bottle of California Merlot. While we waited for the wine Don briefly excused himself to go to the bathroom, so that Michelle and I had a few minutes to chat alone. It was a useful interlude: the two brothers' accounts, combined with Linda's recollections, were still thrumming in my mind, and as I'd had no discussions with anybody except the protagonists I felt in need of some sideline perspective. The only thing that was missing from Don and Dave's punctilious account, charged with honesty was some objectivity about their father. Don's evident veneration and his reluctance to attribute any base motives to him all now linked in with the house's shrinelike interior, the untouched surrounding gardens and, as Don had begun to tell me in the car on our way to the restaurant, his desire to set up a museum around the story of the discovery and of the Arlington art group. Why couldn't he see his father for the faker he was?

Michelle began by recalling the nightly telephone conversations between the brothers, and the escalating pitch of intrigue as their hypothesis began to be fleshed out with real evidence. I then edged her round to the subject of the culprit.

"But what about Don Senior?" I asked. "What type of man was he?"

She answered the question, as I hoped she would, with an observation about his son.

"There's something very strong going on with Don Junior's attitude to his father," she was saying as he reappeared, "and it seems that for the time being he can't get beyond it."

Parentage and provenance share similar powers of supremacy. I have often observed how a painting's story, a tumultuous price or the esteem attaching to a former owner can dictate the perception of a picture's merits, and indeed auctioneers and dealers sometimes rely upon these when setting prices. Don's devotion to his father was as constraining as the most airtight provenance.

This unquestioning reverence has its upside, I reflected, as Don drove me back down the steep mountain road to my hotel and, with my encouragement, continued to sketch out ideas for Arlington's first art museum—an institution for the public good born out of a son's unquestioning love for his father.

CHAPTER 4

The Rembrandt in Disguise

In an old house in Amsterdam lives a professor who wields daunting power in the highest echelons of the art world. His name is Ernst van de Wetering, and he has come to be an arbiter of life or death for the works of Rembrandt van Rijn. Given that Rembrandt is arguably the most famous artist who ever lived, the professor's deliberations are of prodigious consequence. In his capacity as chairman of the Rembrandt Research Project, if he gives your seventeenth-century panel painting the "up" sign, it could be valued at, say, $25 million; should he give it the "down" sign, perhaps as little as a few thousand dollars. Considering that to 99.9 percent of the population both works would look the same, it is easy to see why to many the status of this man is akin to that of a medieval alchemist—a superhuman who can transform base metal into gold or, to put it more prosaically, a musty old painting into a compelling cultural artifact.

In 2003 something greatly heightened my curiosity about Ernst van de Wetering. He had been sharply thrust into the media's glare when a previously overlooked Rembrandt fake, of negligible value, was unmasked as an original to be offered at auction. Asking around I began to piece together one of those absorbing tales of detection and commitment that so often make art-world discoveries more compelling than the ripest fiction, and from which the professor and his team began to emerge with audacious triumph. I have to admit to a personal fascination. The skills he demonstrated go to the core of what I and many others aspire to do for a living; the difference was that here was an establishment intellectual prepared to take daring risks not for any commercial gain but in the exclusive pursuit of truth.

I came to know the name of the picture's owner by chance, from a lucky meeting with a French small-time dealer in old masters at the opening night of a contemporary art exhibition on Bond Street. It was one of the many modern shows thrown by Thomas Williams, an old-master dealer with fine-art training and a flair for promoting new talent to balance a business specializing in the long dead. Having noticed the Frenchman at auctions and other events over the past twenty years, I had marked him as a man well tapped into his native art scene, from where, it was rumored, the picture had recently emanated. His calling card was a richly patterned Scottish tweed suit, cut rather more huggingly than Savile Row would countenance, and I spotted it from across the room. Perhaps he had confused the Pimm's for lemonade as by the time I made my way over to him through the noticeably glamorous multitude that evening, he was drunk. A slice of lemon had tumbled from his glass and lodged itself between his shirt buttons, an observation for which he thanked me before becoming pipingly emotional on the subject of the Rembrandt, which had filled the art press the previous week. He was intoxicatingly keen to unburden himself. The owner, he told me, had been a dealer in *brocante* (bric-a-brac) named Paul Page. He had known the man in the sixties and had even bought some items from him; he also clearly recalled the picture hanging on his wall. If *only* he had acquired it when he'd had the opportunity to do so, he morosely exhaled, his life would have taken a different course. As all ownership details had been held back from the press this nugget was enticing, but I was not keen to play receptacle to either the teetering contents of his glass or his mounting melancholy and chose to call it a night.

Paul Page had bought the painting at a Paris auction in the 1960s, this part of the sale provenance was known, but what I later gathered from others was that he did so with the not uncommon dealer's hope that it might be genuine, that beneath what looked like later additions of jewelry and ornamentation lay an authentic Rembrandt, struggling to free itself from its incarceration by paint. Having secured the work, Page decided to play liberator too. It was, and still is, a common enough practice for dealers at the lower end of the market to avoid costs by restoring paintings themselves, sometimes with disastrous results in the case of sensitive old masters. As I admit in my introduction, I once tried it myself, in the full knowledge that an enthusiastic amateur wielding solvents and blades is about as reassuring as a beautician with a blowtorch. To be fair to Page, however, a previous owner had already begun the process, as evinced by a surviving photograph from the thirties, which showed that the subject had previously sported a faintly farcical red bonnet. Page perilously continued the process by removing yet more detail with a scalpel—namely a pair of gaudy earrings, together with hair and mustache extensions.

Despite some very strange passages in the face, including a solid-looking fish eye, and an unlikely costume, Page's further trimming went some way toward improving its appearance—so much so that he felt ready to requisition the support of an academic authority. In Paris at the time there was one obvious figure who, although not a Rembrandt expert, carried a reputation for exacting connoisseurship: Frederik Lugt. In my gallery we have a number of his volumes on the history of collections and these have proved an invaluable research resource. Frits Lugt, as he was known, was more than just an amasser of invaluable information, however, and it is easy to see why Page would have sought him out in the sixties, for at the end of the previous decade he had helped found the Institut Néerlandais, a bastion of Netherlandish culture in France with the express aim of promoting Dutch literature and the arts to the French public. It also became the home of the Fondation Custodia, a choice collection of paintings, prints and books meticulously collected by Lugt and his wife.

In what circumstances Lugt first viewed the picture is unknown to me, but his response, I discovered, was guardedly encouraging. He did not rule out the possibility that it was by the great master. But, whatever view he might personally have held, he did not have the authority to elevate it, particularly given its compromised state.

In the 1980s, Page and Lugt having died, Page's daughter (whose first name I have not found; had I continued with my inebriated companion I might have done so, but at what cost?) decided to seek the opinion of one Maria van Berghe, the then incumbent director of the Institut Néerlandais. Van Berghe duly sent an image to Josua Bruyn in Amsterdam, who was then one of the most prominent Rembrandt scholars. The response was not heartening. The anointed expert pronounced it a "charming fake."

Still undeterred, a decade and a half later Page's daughter arranged to show the portrait to the new gatekeeper of Rembrandt's work, Ernst van de Wetering. What happened next, with the professor's blessing, was the boldest feat of detection and restoration I had ever heard sanctioned by an eminent academic. The desire to find out more grew irresistible when I heard that the professor, together with his favored restorer, Martin Bijl, had continued to perform these magical operations in their home city of Amsterdam. I was therefore uplifted when, after a couple of unanswered e-mails, the academic colossus finally agreed to grant me an audience the following day and told me that Bijl would also see me. As luck would have it, one of their latest "upgrades"—although somewhat more modest in physical transformation—was on display at the TEFAF antiques fair in Maastricht, so I decided to visit this first and then take the two-hour train journey to Amsterdam.

Maastricht is to the newly cleaned, researched and represented old master what Cannes is to the latest film, and for nine days in March this ancient Roman city becomes a mecca for the art and antiques trade, whose members present the finest objects they have acquired in the previous year; of late it has expanded to include more recent and even contemporary works. The fair is located not in the center of the picturesque medieval market town but among a jumble of modernist buildings in a vast exhibition complex that has forfeited architectural distinction for functionality. Unlike other art and antiques venues, such as Grosvenor House in London or the Armory in New York, its purpose-built efficiency allows exhibitors the freedom of theater designers to express any concept or fantasy best suited to their wares. Some choose painstakingly to reconstruct the interiors of their gallery showrooms back in London, New York, or Paris; others reinvent themselves, go sparsely modernist, or unleash their dreams by cladding their stands in original paneling from French châteaux. Everywhere there are treasures exquisitely lit and labeled, vetted by a crack team of academics, dealers and restorers whose job it is to uphold the reputation of the event and ensure that only the finest and the best can be set before the fair's visitors.

And well they might. For migrating to this feast of annual splendor are some of the world's biggest art buyers and most distinguished eminences: museum directors with their favored patrons, major collectors both young and old, established and new art historians, journalists and writers, as well as a preponderance of dealers. It is the art world's equivalent of the mayfly hatch, when trout unanimously break the surface, and it is there that the annual fortunes of many dealers are decided. As the profit made by the fair organizers is fed back into its running, the event becomes yet more ambitious and better marketed each year. To add a flourish for old-timers who have been visiting since its inception in the mid-1970s, in 2008 the interior was decorated with 175,000 anemones, representing 70 percent of the world's entire cultivated production for the first half of March. The imprint of its enlightened new chairman Ben Janssens, himself a dealer in Oriental works of art, was also evident in a row of mini-stands next to the main restaurant, a new concept for less established dealers of quality who might one day make it into the grand pantheon itself. The city does its best to accommodate the annual event too. The morning I arrived, two days after the fair had opened, the organizers proudly reported that ten thousand people had attended their private view, that every hotel and restaurant had been reserved or filled and that 136 private jets had already flown into the airport (including a private Boeing 707).

Maneuvering my way through the blooms and past some of the 227 exhibitors, a number of whom were friends and colleagues, I finally found the Rembrandt. The proprietor of the stand, Will Noortman, was a youth by art-world standards, a fresh-faced twenty-six-year-old Dutch Old Etonian with swept-back black hair, sporting a slightly burdened look on his fourth day of incoming crowds. His father, Robert, had been a remarkable powerhouse within the art world, determined, driven and inordinately successful, with a particular flair for early Dutch art, but he had died a year earlier, barely months after selling his gallery and stock as a going concern to Sotheby's for what amounted to over $80 million of shares and capital. I found Will seated at a large table in the middle of his capacious stand, behind him, cordoned off with ropes, a seven-inch-high Rembrandt self-portrait around which visitors were constantly collecting.

I recalled too well that midfair feeling as I sat down with him that morning. Although my experiences derive from the art fairs of London and Palm Beach, the endurance course was similar,

and I freely admit to not being good at it: the constant require-
ment to remain vigilant for the transformative big buyer (particularly the one who appears on the first day seemingly ready to
commit but has yet to return); the need to ration energy but be
charming to all; the necessity to listen and be educated as well as
to educate; and the growing awareness of the weight of your
human frame as you stand in preparedness (I now increasingly
sit) three days into a fair that continues for God knows how
much longer, fresh air and daylight dwindling into distant memory. Sometimes the pressure of confinement grows unbearable
and by the last day I have known experienced dealers to flip. At
Palm Beach one year I and some of my colleagues developed an
unhealthy fascination with the face-lift culture. It seemed that
every wealthy female visitor over a certain age had been attended
to by one of two surgeons who based his designs on either Michael
Jackson or the Bride of Wildenstein: spotting the cosmetic master
became a competition requiring some connoisseurship.

Will's stamina buoyantly revived when I asked him about
his star attraction.

"This has been the picture's first Maastricht since it was
rerestored," he explained, looking back at the painting. "We
sold it to a collector and then, following the recent remarkable
transformation, we are reoffering it for the present owner."

Behind his public-school vowels I could not detect even the
faintest Dutch accent; his manner was direct, open and engaging. I could not help feeling that William could one day go some
way toward filling his father's shoes, or at least fashioning a
distinguished pair for himself.

Rembrandt's eighty or so recorded self-portraits have
always been particularly prized by collectors. Not only did

the artist have haunting and, as a young man, romantic looks, but he turned to his own face and body to express his constant explorations into technique and characterization. As Professor van de Wetering had proved, Rembrandt held his self-portraits in stock for clients who wanted both the subject itself—the celebrated artist—and an intrinsic work of genius. Three hundred and fifty years later, the market remains as strong as ever.

The transformations to which William was referring were those to the hat and hand. The diminutive portrait's recent history dated bach to 1997, when it was with a Parisian dealer and considered to be either a copy or the work of a follower. In that year Van de Wetering and his team conclusively declared it a genuine Rembrandt, a significant new addition to the artist's oeuvre and his smallest self-portrait. However, as the professor pondered it more over the following months while working on a major new study of the artist's self-portraits, he became convinced that something was not right: there were anomalies, which he managed to narrow down to the artist's hat and hand. As befitted his proactive style he requested (via Robert Noortman) that the owner allow him to do additional research, and, after intense scientific and art-historical analysis, he suggested that both hat and hand could be removed. The obvious man to do it was the Rembrandt Research Project's expert restorer, Martin Bijl. The picture's owner acceded to the request. Bijl pulled out his solvents and scalpels and got to work, revealing the shadowy remnants of Rembrandt's original hand beneath its prosthetic imposter. The same was done to the hat, which had been fashionably "updated," probably by the same artist around the same time, and it was duly returned to its less voguish original appearance. The Maastricht public was thus now invited to pay tribute to two exciting arrivals: the artist's newly revealed hand and his original hat—or, to quote the gallery literature, "the painting . . . as Rembrandt created it." As I left his stand, William touched on the magnetism that such an object exerts on the wealthy: an original Rembrandt self-portrait, he commented with a smile, has ultimate sex appeal.

Although American museums sometimes deaccession pictures and discoveries are occasionally made, in 2003 Sotheby's worked out that only three Rembrandt self-portraits remained in private hands. This one was on sale for 18 million euros. The twenty-first-century art market had been commercially bountiful for this artist, partly underpinned by high auction prices but also by dealers such as Alfred Bader and Otto Naumann. It often takes no more than one man to boost a market, as had been proved by a forty-five-year-old Wall Street financier named Tom Kaplan, who in the previous few years had managed astonishingly to acquire at least eight original Rembrandts— an almost impossible accomplishment of collecting prowess given the scarcity of available works. The market for authentic Rembrandts was stronger than it had ever been, and to be able to offer at Maastricht a "new" self-portrait courtesy of Professor van de Wetering and his committee was something of a coup.

When a prospective discovery is made, it is of inestimable value to secure the support of a recognized expert to endorse your claim. However great the dealer's or auctioneer's knowledge may be, and likewise his or her integrity, we occupy a commercial theater, and the reassurance of objective academia offers a further layer of comfort to clients. Almost all deceased artists of stature have a man or woman on earth who is prepared to act as an arbiter of authenticity, and they come in all shapes and sizes.

Some have become so by dint of a formal position, such as the directorship of a museum or the curatorship of a major national institution, particularly if the institution's holdings include works by the artist in question; more commonly, authority comes from having published on the artist (there are few better places to have the last word than on the platform of a scholarly book or two); and sometimes clout is derived simply from a consensus of regard among academics, auctioneers and dealers. In France the heir of the artist who has rights to the estate will sometimes assume this position, and Picasso, Matisse and Pissarro all have family descendants recognized by the art establishment. For all art experts, once their position is recognized by the leading dealers and auction houses, there are two tangible benefits: the opportunity to keep abreast of anything new in their sector, and the chance, in some instances, to be paid for their expertise.

I have an enormous regard for many of these experts. There are, however, grave weaknesses in the system when the expert is not up to the task, and these have proved both frustrating and also, to make up for it, extremely beneficial. Take a hypothetical scenario. You are an academic who has decided to write a book on a valuable artist; you have a series of well-regarded qualifications, including perhaps a doctorate or professorship, and soon find a willing publisher. You decide to take an angle that will interest people—this could be anything from the painter's preoccupation with sex, attitudes to feminism (a common favorite), politics, or other artists, and so on. The book is favorably reviewed in the academic and possibly popular press, and you are approached by a museum to curate an exhibition on the artist. You also give lectures, teach, and write articles, and soon find you are the preeminent art historian on the subject.

Sir Anthony Van Dyck (1599–1641), *Lady Mary Villiers*

OIL ON CANVAS • 42 X 33" • 101.6 X 83.8CM

Hidden behind the relined canvas of this distinguished Van Dyck
portrait we found the royal brand, which proved unequivocally that
it had belonged to King Charles I, whose art collection was dispersed
after his execution in 1649.

royal brand on *Lady Mary
Villiers* by Sir Anthony
Van Dyck

OIL ON CANVAS • 42 X 33" •
101.6 X 83.8CM

Rembrandt van Rijn (1606–1669), Hidden self-portrait

OIL ON PANEL • 28.87 X 21.73" • 70.8 X 55.2CM

The Page portrait as it began life, from a photograph taken at the beginning of the century, when the painting was replete with additions made in Rembrandt's studio.

The picture as Page bought it. As can be seen, the previous owner had by then already removed the upright bonnet.

The portrait after Page had removed the earrings and some of the hair.

Martin Bijl's intensive restoration turned an almost unsaleable hybrid, with its unappealing fish eye, into a work executed solely by Rembrandt, which later sold for £7 million.

Ernst van de Wetering and Martin Bijl

Professor Ernst Van der Wetering, one of the art world's most respected and influential connoisseurs, is head of the Rembrandt Research Project. On his left is the Amsterdam-based Project's eminent restorer, Martin Bijl, with whom he has worked and collaborated on many Rembrandtian quests and discoveries.

Ernst Van de Wetering (1938–), *Portrait of My Father*

Turning momentarily from analysis to creation, Professor Van der Wetering produced an intriguing picture in which he is seen as a child watching his father painting.

Anglo-Flemish School c.1500.
Portrait of Arthur Prince of Wales (1486–1502)

OIL ON PANEL • 11 X 7" • 28 X 18CM

One of my first significant discoveries: the only provable contemporary
portrait of the first heir to the Tudor throne.

Sixteenth-century English School,
Young Elizabeth c. 1547–1558

OIL ON PANEL • 30 X 15" • 76.2 X 38.1CM

Formerly thought to be a later copy, this contemporary portrait of Princess (later Queen) Elizabeth was, through painstaking restoration, dramatically revealed beneath several campaigns of later restoration.

Dr. Bendor Grosvenor

Historian, indefatigable researcher and crucial collaborator in numerous picture-hunting and buying ventures.

Attributed to the Dutch artist "Steven," the *Hampden Portrait of Elizabeth I*, c. 1563

OIL ON PANEL, LAID ONTO CANVAS • 77 ¼ X 55 ¼" • 196 X 140 CM

Our great purchase, after cleaning. Following removal of unnecessary overpaint, the portrait thrillingly regained much of its lost luster, quality and detail. Subsequent research added the rest, including a new appraisal of the artist "Steven."

This rose with oak leaves, painted by a different hand and at a later date than the original work, sparked intriguing conjectures.

Lansdowne manusript, c. 1563

The handwritten manuscript for a speech Queen Elizabeth I gave to the House of Lords in 1563 in which she referred to tree blossoms, fruit and ripeness. These themes are echoed in the portrait we bought.

Roadshow catch

This group of pictures arrived on my table at the *Antiques Roadshow* on May 22, 2008, at Althorp Castle in Northamptonshire. All six had been found next to a dump by a lucky fisherman in Youghal, southern Ireland.

Winslow Homer (1836–1910), *Children under a Palm*, 1885

WATERCOLOR AND PENCIL ON PAPER • 12 x 20" • 25.6 x 50.8CM

The best of the catch: a lost watercolor by one of America's greatest nineteenth-century artists that took me to Ireland, New York and the Bahamas in search of clues to its subject and the circumstances of its creation.

Now take the prospective purchaser's viewpoint. You are offered by a dealer, or persuaded to bid on by an auctioneer, a newly discovered work by this artist. It is not in any of the established literature, it may have been dirty or with overpaint—perhaps still is—and lacks any useful provenance. The price being asked is commensurate with those that the artist has achieved before, but it requires a hefty check, so you want some comfort that what is claimed is true. You have fallen for the painting, however, and would not like to lose the opportunity to acquire it. Unless the dealer's or auctioneer's expertise and reputation are such that no other endorsement is required, the most obvious thing is to go to, or ask for the picture to be seen by, the perceived expert. Googling that person's name, you find it ubiquitously flagged next to the artist's.

Imagine once again that you are the expert. The query arrives by e-mail, together with an invitation to view the picture in the flesh. Quite right they should send it to you, given the large chunk of your life you have devoted to the artist: a man or woman whom you have studied with all the available means at your disposal, almost every recorded major work of whom you have seen (the rest as photos), and about whom you know every theory proposed.

The first hurdle is that you need to see the painting in the flesh—few if any experts would risk offering a conclusive opinion from a photograph. If the painting happens to be on the other side of the world there is an immediate logistical and cost issue: either it must come to you, or you must go to it. But even with the benefit of a full physical inspection, you know your limitations. As a result of your researches, you are aware that the artist has been faked in the past, that he had followers and studio assistants. You therefore heed an inner voice of caution.

You could speak for an hour on the subject matter—if indeed it is by the artist in question—but what about the physicality of the work of art? Can you really understand the condition? Do you *really* know the idiosyncratic traits of the artist, as opposed to those of people who were highly influenced by him or whom he taught? Have you fully understood his qualities in the context of the numerous apes, pretenders and copyists—the only true way of reading the fingerprint? The work is also atypical in both subject and style (which was why it was discovered in the first place), so it requires an even greater reliance on your eye and intuition.

You have to fall back on *connoisseurship*—the skill of defining and recognizing the strokes of the master on the basis of what is before you. Are you *really* the person for this? Your knowledge of the artist's life and subject matter is unparalleled, but when it comes to the minutiae of technique, can you confidently shift from the theoretical to the physical? Your acclaimed book did not require this type of insight, nor did your broader training in art history. Curating the exhibition was very valuable experience, but it was more to prove a thesis than provide an overview of the artist's techniques. What's more, do you sense this carries the risk of exposure, that there is money involved? What do you therefore say? The best course may be to vacillate: you could just describe it as *possibly by*—at least that way you will not expose yourself to the risks of a commercial transaction as much as if you say definitely yes or no. But there again perhaps it is right, and you are irresponsibly ruling out what could be a new work by your chosen artist. And so on and so forth.

Art history and connoisseurship are in my view separate disciplines that sometimes combine, but not always: a military historian does not necessarily make a good general, a professor of economics a good businessman. They both have the capacity to be so, and can certainly talk the talk if required, but they are different fields of human competence.

The upside to this is that paintings that are manifestly authentic, but have been turned down, can sometimes be bought at auction for a fraction of their true value. They are the classic "sleepers." The auctioneers of the miscatalogued Rembrandt I mentioned in the introduction state that it was checked out by the Rijksmuseum in Amsterdam and a major auction house before the sale. The downside is that if you do find something unequivocally genuine, the experts may not have the skills, confidence or time to endorse it. Of course you could say this is the moan of any would-be discoverer, but there are occasions when the proof is so plain to see, the characteristics so redolent of the artist in question, the circumstantial evidence so compelling, that even a blind dog with a stick can see them. These travesties normally have a way of sorting themselves out with time—art history moves on, new academics get involved, the expert develops connoisseurship—but time is a luxury in a fast-moving, competitive world with biting bank loans and gallery overheads.

I know of experts who are erratic, emotionally driven, bombastic and political, some of them with prestigious publishing commissions, who can obscure the proper understanding of an artist by their limitations and prejudices. I know of one case where an academic told the incredulous owner of a picture, "I know who painted this, but why should I tell you so you can make money" (admittedly the academic was not in this instance being paid for his expertise). There are also great art historians whose pronouncements close the case, even though convincing evidence to the contrary emerges. Although technological and art-historical knowledge lessen the scope for cardinal errors, as long as the attribution relies on the judgment of a human this phenomenon will remain.

I had arranged to meet Professor van de Wetering at the Rembrandt House, a priceless remnant of old Amsterdam which has the distinction of having been the home where for nineteen years the artist lived and worked, and also, by one of those historical flukes following his unavoidable bankruptcy in midcareer (during a liquidity crunch), of having had all its original furnishings and chattel documented in minute detail. Using the bankruptcy filings as a guide, the Dutch faithfully reconstructed the interior with seventeenth-century furniture, objects and paintings (some of which hung there originally) with the same care and reverence in evidence at Anne Frank's hidden apartment a few streets away.

I arrived early for my appointment and spent an hour looking through the menagerie of pictures, plaster casts, sculptures and artifacts from the kitchen upward, many in the same position they had occupied in Rembrandt's day, because the inventories had identified items by location too. Rembrandt was an art dealer as well as a painter, and the large building was not merely a home to live and paint in but a place in which to entertain and do business, for he sold not just his own paintings and prints, but also works by pupils, assistants and other artists whose work he admired. For a period he had a thriving business supplying and producing art for the connoisseurs of Holland, employing a coterie of helpers to replicate, copy and adapt; despite the dislocations of time and history, and the dead hand of the health and safety regulations that all museums must observe, the faint hum of seventeenth-century industry can still be imagined as one explores the house.

On the ground floor I took a moment to survey the book shop, heaving with publications on Amsterdam's artistic legend. Ernst van de Wetering's name featured almost as ubiquitously as Rembrandt's. The sight of all this scholarship and the thought of the scantness of the research I had undertaken in London made me feel a little uneasy. How, I began to wonder, would I fare in conversation with so formidable a man about an artist who was far from my specialist subject?

The princes of art history can be intolerant of ignorance, particularly when it results from a lack of knowledge of their own publications. I fully remember one to whom I showed a picture while at university who told me to bugger off and read the second chapter of his book before he would resume the conversation. I am still smarting from the redress twenty-five years on. That formidable scholar, the late Sir Oliver Millar, whom we met in the introduction, had a courtly demeanor that could also be graciously withering, and as a younger dealer I would sometimes make use of his encyclopedic knowledge of British houses, collections and their ancestries to deflect direct discussion of attributions, particularly if the picture was in poor condition, which he had a tendency to respond to as artistic shortfall. His forte was to swamp our discussion with a torrent of comparable examples "of which of course you will be aware, Mr. Mould."

I knew that Ernst van de Wetering had been involved with Rembrandt for forty years, since the Dutch government's decision in 1968 to support a committee of establishment art historians under the name of the Rembrandt Research Project. The idea was proposed by two art historians, Professor Josua Bruyn (the same man whose opinion had been sought by Page's daughter) and Bob Haak, director of the Amsterdam Historical

Museum. This was strikingly innovative, and the first time an authentication committee had been established for a deceased painter. In fact its establishment was deemed essential, for an implausible number of paintings were knocking around that were said to be by the nation's greatest artist, largely because there had been (and still is) a tendency to mistake for authentic original works by talented assistants and followers who deliberately aped their master's techniques and style. The Van Gogh Museum, following the RRP's example, has since taken a similar approach. Such comprehensive art-historical analysis could greatly benefit a number of other internationally renowned painters whose works are often subject to such mistakes: I would personally like to see more inclusive forums for some of Britain's leading painters, notably Gainsborough and Constable, but the requirements of this approach are not without problems, as the RRP itself discovered in its early days.

In 1905, when the first serious Rembrandt catalogue was attempted, there were believed to be close to six hundred original Rembrandts in the world (this figure has now been reduced to about 330) and although by the time the committee began its work this number had been whittled down, there was still a lot of confusion between the ducks and the swans. Ernst van de Wetering was present from the outset, although his initial attachment was largely a fluke. Reading his CV, you would hardly describe him as the classic art historian the RRP's founders would have had in mind for the job. The son of a Dutch technical designer and a German mother, he trained as an artist at the Hague Royal Academy and then taught art at a secondary school, but at the age of twenty-three he decided to throw it in and travel through Italy, Egypt and Greece. In Greece he bought and journeyed around on a donkey to complete what, in his idiosyncratic way, he perceived as an authentic native experience. There this explorative bohemian met up with two German intellectuals who so fired him with academic enthusiasm that after another spell of teaching he decided to go to Amsterdam University to study philosophy, only to find he lacked the necessary classical qualifications. Much to his chagrin, he was obliged to pursue art history instead. A noticeably accomplished artist, before he finished his bachelor's degree he spent six months in Brooklyn, New York, where he carved his own panel supports for his paintings and ground his own colors in focused seclusion—a taste of the compulsive investigations he was later to apply to Rembrandt.

At twenty-nine Van de Wetering was invited to temporarily assist the fledgling Rembrandt Research Project by its then chairman, Josua Bruyn. Van de Wetering's job, that of a student assistant, was fairly menial to start with and involved planning research trips for the committee and assembling the necessary documentation; it was not well paid and he supplemented his income by tapping another of his gifts, the ability to play the flute, clarinet and piccolo, which he did in the evenings for professional orchestras. It was not long, however, before his visual talents were noticed by the professors of the RRP. This partly came about because one of the committee members fell ill and someone was required to fill his place; the young administrator was therefore temporarily requisitioned. Able now to contribute more conspicuously, he was quickly perceived to have a peculiarly powerful eye born of an artist's practical insight. A formal position was soon crafted for him within Amsterdam's Central Research Laboratory for Objects of Art and Science, where he would work for almost two decades. It was a fortuitous placement for all concerned. With Van de Wetering embedded among some of the brightest art restorers and scientists, not only did the RRP now have a sound technical underpinning for its investigations, but the hippie turned art historian could begin to foment his own potent blend of eclectic connoisseurship.

The appointment brought another benefit: it equipped Van de Wetering with the moral courage to go further in seeking out answers than many art historians had felt comfortable doing. During this period he gradually raised his profile and became an internationally regarded expert in the theory and ethics of conservation and restoration; for six years he coordinated a working group for the International Council of Museums. This new brand of academic study, in which he became a leader, partly focused on the controversial principles of how far it was acceptable to go in returning an artifact to its original appearance. Van de Wetering acquired the acknowledged authority that he was later daringly to wield as the RRP's chairman.

The committee's members had set about their work with the zeal of the Spanish Inquisition, traveling in pairs, traversing the world to cross-question every claimant. They developed a tendency to come to conclusions by group consensus using old-fashioned techniques of connoisseurship. In other words, they established a concept of what a Rembrandt should look like, and individual paintings were branded either "right" or "wrong," or occasionally accorded a "don't know." Howls of grief and shock were heard in some of the greatest stately homes and museums as news came through that their hallowed Rembrandt had been given the thumbs down. It even happened at Buckingham Palace, where the Queen was told that her esteemed Rembrandt *Bust of a Young Man in a Turban* was instead by his apprentice, Isaac de Jouderville. The process was cold-blooded and in some instances unduly restrictive, but few dared to question the verdict.

By 1989, working chronologically, the RRP had published three volumes, with considerably more to come. Although integral to the project from its inception, Van de Wetering was beginning to feel unhappy. He had spent eighteen years attached to the laboratory, analyzing the techniques, considering the functions of sketches, immersing himself in the theories of art of Rembrandt's time, as well as in studio practices and fashions, and realized that a different approach was required. He saw paintings as a "process" and attribution as crucially dependent on a group of supportive arguments from various academic disciplines.

With youth on his side (the old guard were by now peeling off) and a formidable group of collaborators from a diverse set of disciplines, among them the fashion historian Marieke de Winkel, the restorer Martin Bijl, the scientist Karin Groen and the dendrochronologist Peter Klein, as well as experts in archival research, handwriting, etching and drawing, in 1993 Van de Wetering raised his standard as the new chairman of the Rembrandt Research Project. "Connoisseurship," he announced in the *Burlington Magazine*, the leading academic publication dedicated to art, "will be deployed with the greatest possible reserve and only when all other arguments have been exhausted." The art world sat up and listened. He is not without his critics, including respected art historians who have challenged his approach, but, following the publication in 2007 of the RRP's fourth volume, very many continue to believe that Van de Wetering's committee and its dramatic advances—not least brave revisions of some of the previous committee's pronouncements—have gone further than anyone else in rationalizing and codifying the art and science of attribution. In the case of the Page self-portrait the RRP's joint disciplines and expertise had elevated a misshapen duck to a swan.

I t was late afternoon by the time I checked in with the receptionist at the museum, and she told me that the professor would meet me up on the third floor. As I exited the lift a group of what I assumed were Rembrandt-owning hopefuls of Middle Eastern appearance were being shown out. I saw that I was now at the center of a living process, the place where Rembrandt's legacy must so often have been considered, adjudicated and discussed. A Dutchman who had been hosting the group turned to me. He had a plump, Falstaffian appearance with white, curly hair and round glasses, but what gave his face distinction was its classically shaped mouth, which I immediately recognized from the dust jackets in the museum bookshop. Professor van de Wetering welcomed me with a hurried smile, offered me his hand, and then briskly led me off into a large and quite modern general office, filled with desks, screens and books, which contrasted starkly with the interior of the museum—with one notable exception: somewhat incongruously propped on the floor were two Rembrandtesque paintings on low easels. The professor explained that one belonged to the Tel Aviv collectors who had just left, the other to a Miami collector, and then he went straight to the point.

"I thought I might show you the sort of thing I'm frequently obliged to consider. Two paintings of similar subjects that show the workings of his studio assistants—"satellite paintings," we call them—variants of the master's originals, which he encouraged." His ability to express complexity with clarity in a language not native to him was impressive. Throwing a look around the museum's nerve center, he was clearly concerned that our discussions would disturb the staff, so before we got any deeper he suggested that we go somewhere else, where we could talk more freely.

This, it turned out, was the building next door, Rembrandt Corner, the house where Rembrandt first lived when he came to Amsterdam. It was also a bar, and Van de Wetering admitted he could do with a drink. We found a corner table overlooking a canal, a waxwork figure of Rembrandt above us, leering like an aging fairground prop. Ernst, as I was now told to call him, speedily ordered beer and a plate of meatballs dipped in bread crumbs, which were set down next to the weighty volumes he had brought from the museum. Thus installed and ready to talk, he visibly relaxed. Within minutes this curious amalgam of artist, academic and, as I was to discover, disarmingly potent romantic became human. I was not there to see him with a picture to authenticate, my normal reason for visiting such pedagogues, but in a sense almost the reverse—for him to explain to me how he saw and understood painting and how he had achieved the insights that had brought him and his committee their extraordinary status.

Unless they are challenged introverts, art historians generally learn to converse with a wider public, not least because of the need to persuade their publishers, fellow scholars and students of their theories. Van de Wetering, it rapidly became clear, had elevated this power of communication to an art form. As he sipped his beer and nibbled on his meatballs he lured me into his subject with unusual charisma and conviction. He began by speaking of Rembrandt the prodigy, the most intelligent and adventurous artist in Holland, an artistic giant thrillingly discovered in his native town of Leiden by young intellectuals who identified in him the promise so sought in the Renaissance to "surpass the achievements of antiquity." He had set the scene like the introduction to a great historical novel, yet all he had really done was to allude to the conclusions of contemporary art writers such as Karel van Mander and Samuel van Hoogstraten, in whose works he was immersed. If you know about Rembrandt's time, the society in which he worked and the patrons who fed him, he explained, his art becomes more comprehensible, and individual works more attributable.

"He reinvented painting," Ernst continued, now in stride. "Rembrandt took every aspect and scrutinized it: space, light, drapery, human proportions, attitudes, composition, reflection of light. One of his great miracles was his use of paint, how he used it to imbue the painting with life. His risks and inclusion of chance items become bolder and bolder; it is a process that brings him closer to nature, and in a way the painting paints itself!" He had moved his beer and opened a book before him, gesturing to the thick, complex layers of paint applied with abstract wildness in a late composition. Rarely had I heard someone talk about seventeenth-century painting in such startlingly fresh terms or, for that matter, with such passion and confidence. He had turned the pages to an early self-portrait that I immediately recognized as the restored Page portrait. His insights now became more conspiratorial.

"Notice how the light from the nose and cheekbone reflect into the eye socket," he said. "This can be described as a *traffic of light*, an example of Rembrandt's utter sophistication. The normal beholder does not question the means of illusion. If the illusion is successful by definition you do not see its means—but it's the means that create the effect. By examining his art in this way, it gives us a greater vocabulary—and with that comes articulation, and the power of argument."

It was masterful advocacy, born of indefatigable observation and reflection, the sort of incisive seeing and deconstructing that lies at the heart of devastating connoisseurship. He had mastered a way of conveying his subject's genius in that electrifying way with which I have seen great teachers win over and inspire their students for life.

Eventually, at my insistence, we moved from Rembrandt to Van de Wetering and he talked about his youth, his early desire to be a philosopher, and his love of Goethe and the German Romantics. We also discussed his home life and how he had divorced, then remarried, only to marry his first wife again in later life. The couple now lived on separate floors of their tall Amsterdam house. Such was Ernst's candor that I felt confident enough to broach a topic that particularly fascinated me: how he squared his life's work with the huge financial consequences of his deliberations. This allowed me to go on to raise the subject of the Page portrait. I hit a nerve. His expression tightened.

"Money gets in the way of your perception of art. If you want to buy a sonata by Schubert you can do so for ten euros and with it a whole collection of others by him. A Shakespeare sonnet costs you nil. Great art should be everybody's, but the problem is that concepts of rarity and originality can block perception.

The eye is disturbed by the aura of authenticity when looking at the original. This is why I greatly support the idea of popular reproductions, as they remove you from this."

"But how," I asked, "do you square all this with your power? Whether you like it or not, your pronouncements can have the effect of turning water into wine—or the reverse. Does it not daunt or compromise you?"

"I have tried to follow the cues of the Romantic movement," he said. "To live life honestly, to trust my own emotions and get closer to the truth. This is what carries me and I never involve myself with the money. Value makes me sick. I hate TEFAF and the art market—in fact I actively seek naivety."

I couldn't recall how much I had told him about my own art dealing but considered it prudent to keep the subject out of our discussion. I was even beginning to question it myself.

"We all have the right to be naïve," he went on. "It gives us the freedom to get back to art and its purpose. Once I was charged for driving off a motorway along the hard shoulder towards the exit. I do not drive much and did so innocently because I was in a traffic jam and thought it would bring relief to the other drivers. A truck driver blocked my way until a policeman came along and fined me. I contested it in court, pointing out that all I was doing was trying to help. And yet they took me for a hard-shoulder bandit! The judge put it to me that I was behaving naïvely. 'But it is your job, sir, to protect my naivety!' I replied. Neither now, nor then, do I feel guilty for my action, because I was assisting others."

Ernst smiled as he ended the story and I got the impression I was not the first to hear it. Taking another sip of beer, he looked out the window to the canal opposite and was silent for a moment before turning to me with a look of sober reflection.

"Truth is of the utmost importance to me. This is what drives me. Until I was fifty I was afraid of telling people my secret."

"Your secret?" I asked, wondering whether I had missed something in our earlier conversation or overlooked some crucial fact in my background research.

"Yes, that for forty years of my life I thought that my father had been a Nazi."

"A Nazi?" I replied, playing down my surprise. "But I thought your father was a Dutchman." Our encounter was moving into a realm I could never have anticipated. With Anne Frank's house close by it was easy to understand the enormity of Ernst's revelation. Even today the occasional German tourist returns to his car to find it scratched by Dutchmen who have long and painful memories of the Nazi occupation of their homeland.

"He joined the NSB, the Dutch National Socialist movement," Ernst continued unabashed. "He was one of the many who were impressed by Hitler's rebuilding of Germany but also, like other Dutchmen, he believed it would prevent the Netherlands from becoming a part of the German Reich. In 1944 my German mother fled Holland to avoid reprisals but Father stayed behind, following us to Germany in 1945. He was then arrested as a Nazi suspect by the British while sketching the little harbor of our village—they assumed he was a spy. After four years in various prison camps he was finally freed, which allowed us to return home. But during the forty years of my life between 1948 and 1998 I concealed the painful secret that he had been a member of that party. It automatically stigmatized him, all of us, as devils! It was a huge relief when I decided to tell people—it allowed me not to be afraid of anything anymore. It is how I seek to lead my life.

"As it happens, however, some of my fears were unfounded. I later got access to the files and it turned out that he had never harmed anybody, nor had he been found guilty of any treason or collaboration. It was his membership in that party—and the fact that he had been allowed to keep his radio—that deeply irritated the tribunal!"

By this time I felt there was no subject I could not broach. I had also noticed that two and a half hours had passed and I had still not properly addressed the Page self-portrait. Now, as I began, he was totally prepared for my questions, and in his response was a flicker of pride too.

"As you know, it had been turned down as a 'charming fake' by my predecessor, Josua Bruyn," he told me. "It was 1995 and this time round I insisted to the owners that if we were going to relook at it we needed the full scientific team in place—the dendrochronologist, the X-ray man, the paint sampler. When they first showed it to me I remember thinking that it looked like a Rembrandt—and then it didn't, because although the right eye, the chin, the nose, the contours were convincing, the rest was not. After two days of intensive analysis I was satisfied that it was a work produced during Rembrandt's lifetime and that the signature looked authentic."

At this stage his research into Rembrandt's studio practices proved invaluable. His ingenious hypothesis (which he was later to write up) that these self-portraits were stock items in Rembrandt's art-dealing operation explained a course of events by which a genuine self-portrait could have turned into the work of a follower within his own lifetime. Under instruction or supervision from Rembrandt himself, his pupils could have either "updated" the features to reflect the maturer man or converted them into a *tronie*, a fun-looking character head with more decorative or commercial appeal, in this case an exotic Russian. Rembrandt had an art business to run, and a little upgrading of his own work here and there made sense for a shopkeeper wishing to stay abreast of the whims of his fashionable clientele.

"As the additions had already been partly removed, this added to our thinking, particularly as we had on file the photograph from the 1930s showing how it was," Ernst continued. "Under normal circumstances we would never advocate undoing part of a painting's history, but there was a valid ethical argument in this case as radical interventions—in the form of previous paint removals—had already taken place, leaving it looking like a hybrid caricature. I told the owner not to sell the painting but to find a partner who would go through the process of restoration and investigation. As we wanted the scholarly benefit of it I offered to supervise. Martin Bijl, who ended up undertaking the restoration, was the perfect man for the job— he has guts and sensitivity and a great love and understanding of Rembrandt."

I had arranged to see Bijl the following day, and before we ended our conversation I asked Ernst about his own art. He proceeded to describe a convoluted composition he was working on of *himself* watching his *father* painting in the German village in which they had lived before returning to Amsterdam—where his father had been with the family for only one week before his arrest by the British. In fact he had the watercolor that his father had painted hanging at home. At my request he did a rapid sketch of the composition, including the eyelines of himself observing his father. As he prepared to leave I could not help but consider the significance of this and felt sufficiently emboldened to hazard an interpretation.

"Given that your life's work has been about getting to the truth of authorship and attribution, your picture is unusually revealing, is it not?"

He was now standing up to go. "You could say that, I suppose," he replied with a whimsical smile, leaving me with an ambiguous sense of only half hitting the mark. Donning his coat and placing the heavy tomes under his arm, the great professor disappeared into the night.

I never had the opportunity to speak to Paul Page's daughter, but after she showed the painting to Ernst in 1995 there followed what can only be described as inertia, for nothing progressed for five years. Then, one morning in 2000, Nicolas Joly, head of Sotheby's Old Master Paintings department in Paris, was asked to come down from his office on rue du Faubourg Saint-Honoré to meet a lady who had brought in a picture. He recalls that it was pure luck that he happened to be there as she had made no appointment and he is often out. But when she removed her wares from an unpromising white plastic bag, Joly, accustomed to assessing all manner of pictures in his job as the auction house's representative, reacted instantly: here was something exciting and to be taken seriously. He arranged for it to be sent to the London office, where it was next seen by George Gordon, a senior figure at the auction house and an expert in seventeenth-century Dutch art. He recalls that two of his colleagues, Alex Bell and Arabella Chandos, were present at the first encounter.

"I remember thinking, this looks like nothing on earth,"

George said. "It was an absolute mess. Looking at it more care-fully, however, I began to notice passages of quality, so I placed a piece of cardboard to cover the problematic upper portions of the face and could see that the lower levels looked real." At this point he had no idea that Van de Wetering had expressed an interest in the picture's destiny and was relying entirely on his subjective response.

"We then sent it to Amsterdam and much to my surprise Ernst van de Wetering told me he had been expecting the pic-ture to return. I had no idea he had seen it!"

Sotheby's thus became a partner in the owner's ambitions to restore and conserve the picture, and the painting made its way to Martin Bijl—arguably the Netherlands' most celebrated conservator of old masters, himself a member of the Rembrandt Research Project and one of the few people in the world suffi-ciently versed in the artist to perform the restoration equivalent of open-heart surgery.

Bijl lives on the outskirts of Alkmaar, known as the cheese town of the Netherlands, in a large house and studio camou-flaged from the outside to look more like a garage than a dwell-ing, with the further security precaution of having no address. I was momentarily fazed when, having arrived at the railway station, I saw an athletic-looking man in his early fifties with Caravaggesque good looks, a thick head of white curls and heavy, black-framed designer glasses draw up in a brand-new Range Rover. On reflection I had pictured this renowned restorer as a boffin rather than a man of magazine-model allure, but, as I was to find out, he was another of these maverick fig-ures whose trajectory into the rarefied world of Rembrandt detection could hardly have been foretold.

Bijl's father was a professional soldier who had worked for one of the country's leading professional football clubs. Despite his young son's manifest interest in drawing and making and repairing models, he distrusted artists, whom he bracketed with homosexuals as corrosive. Art was not allowed in the house, nor was there a radio, for Martin's father thought that pop music was a weapon sent by the Russians to corrupt the young. If Martin returned home just one minute after 10 P.M. he was savagely punished with a prolonged grounding. Unsurprisingly, having done his best for years to survive this horribly oppressive environment, at the age of seventeen he escaped to Amsterdam, where he trained in nursing and worked at a hospital for six years, marrying the most beautiful female nurse on his shift. He spent much of his free time visiting Amsterdam's museums, where his devotion to the work of old masters began to take shape. This pastime grew into a driving urge to work among them, so he wrote to the chief restorer at the Rijksmuseum, the country's leading museum, suggesting that they should meet. Along with observations about modern restoration, he laced his letter with humorous asides. Fortunately the chief restorer both had a sense of humor and liked Martin's approach and offered him a traineeship.

This life-changing break immediately brought with it severe practical problems, as it meant Martin had to give up his day job as a nurse at a time when his pregnant wife had stopped working. Yet he had no doubt whatsoever as to where his destiny lay. Rather like Ernst van de Wetering, he fell back on his alternative resources for survival, finding work as a male catwalk model and as a part-time translator for the local football club during the European Cup.

One of his first tasks at the Rijksmuseum was to touch in the paint losses in a portrait that had been terrifyingly torn down the middle, including the face. For a new boy, he acquitted himself with skill and after two months was offered an unsalaried post within the department. Two years later he began a permanent job at the museum and his career as a restorer took off. He spent the next two decades at the Rijksmuseum, the second as its chief restorer. In January 2000 he made the decision to go out on his own, bringing the benefits of his prodigious experiences to a wider art world and market.

Bijl had used much of his time at the museum to get to know other departments, realizing that only by assiduously studying the artists he was working on, and getting to know the preoccupations of the other experts and specialists, would he be able to make real progress. It was an exciting time in the world of restoration: alongside a growing appetite for reversing the effects of overpainting and damage to get closer to the artist's original idea, there was an increasing desire to understand the nature of the original paints, how they were applied and what they were made from, to get at the atmospheric effects sought by the great masters, often obscured by accidents of history and the passage of time. He recalls explosions of black smoke and oil as he and his colleagues strove for greater insights into the chemical constituents of the painters' mediums. Under Van de Wetering's supervision he made a menu of his discoveries, thereby adding considerably to the understanding of old-master techniques. Bijl's particular interest was base supports, in particular the use of wood, and this gave him a useful extra dimension when it came to Rembrandt, who habitually used wooden panels for moderately sized paintings.

"It was a very special occasion when the picture arrived," Bijl told me. He had taken me along a dimly lit corridor and we were sitting in his office with its many shelves of art books. I was fascinated to behold the other side of the Van de Wetering process: dressed from head to toe in black, Bijl leaned back in his chair with relaxed composure, the off-duty Dionysian, the man with guts who had paired up with the renegade philosopher to push the boundaries of research. This is what made the whole undertaking so novel and edgy. An academic can theorize as much as he likes about what might have been, what could be, what should be, but the combination of Van de Wetering's penetrating insights and the efforts of a man dedicated to putting theory to the test—with irreversible consequences—was spectacularly original.

"Ernst had told me that he was going to send me a painting, and when it arrived and I took it partly out of the crate, I thought, What on earth has he brought me now? What has he done this time? Before I began to recognize passages of high quality, I remember my response being one of confusion, particularly as I looked at its very strange eye, making me even wonder if it was seventeenth-century at all. Ernst phoned me the next day, urged me to continue my analysis, and I expressed to him my highest and lowest expectations."

This strange new arrival now sitting on an easel in his studio, Bijl began to collect his thoughts. Page's painted additions, or touch-ups, as well as those from the earlier restorer who had removed the hat, made it difficult to read what lay beneath those areas. Using a microscope, Bijl noticed manifestly ancient overpaint covering areas of the face and saw that the garments appeared to have been repainted at the same time. The Rembrandt committee's collaborators had furnished him with a file of technical data that included X-rays, reflectograms (to pick up drawing lines beneath the surface) and dendrochronology reports, but as is sometimes the case, apart from providing confirmation that the panel was the appropriate date for a Rembrandt, none of this information was of great assistance to the challenge ahead. What had been applied to the eye and dress was so early, so thick and so indivisible from the lower layer that it had resisted radiographic investigation.

The turning point in Bijl's deliberations came when Van de Wetering sent him photographs of the picture before Page had owned it. His mission up until this point had been to try to understand *why* it had been treated in this way, and by studying the photos he could see how these amputations of the hat and hair were crude attempts at moving the painting toward a mainstream concept of what a Rembrandt *should* look like. It also licensed him to embark on the first, and uncontroversial, stage of removing the twentieth-century overpaint to reveal how these operations were achieved. His findings were telling: the hat had been entirely removed using solvents, the earrings and hair had been barbered with a blade: the scar tissue of both campaigns remained.

These "unthoughtful actions," as he described them, offered an important ethical argument for anything he might consider doing next. As he looked at the portrait now, stripped of its twentieth-century cosmetics, he felt that these early attempts at paint removal had reduced its appearance to a clumsy anomaly. Its present state did not of course answer the fundamental question of what lay beneath the rest of the early additions: it could have been left unfinished, for example, or horribly damaged, but at least he could now work out how it had suffered during the twentieth century.

Indisputably the most ecstatic and occasionally horrifying occasions for me as an art dealer have been when a picture that has been overpainted or partly hidden by opaque layers of dirty varnish is first "opened" to provide a glimpse of what might lie beneath. The hours I have spent looking over the shoulders of my restorers as they work must add up to many months. At such times I witness the destiny of paintings that I may have bought with a strong hunch, sometimes for very considerable sums, gradually unfold with the insistent application of solvents and scalpels. The big question in the case of overpaint is always, why has the picture been treated in this way in the first place, and what surprises lie hidden? I once had the shock of discovering that beneath the overpainted body of an eighteenth-century soldier by Reynolds, for which I had paid dearly, there was nothing but the pumiced remains of his red uniform, rendering it near worthless. The process of overpaint removal can be highly perilous, and one reason why the areas of the eye and face might have been left untouched was possibly, wisely, fear. Facial features are often finished in vulnerable glazes that can be lost with the slightest excess application of scalpel or chemicals.

Bijl was rightly nervous. The last thing he wanted was to turn, by his irreversible actions, an already wounded picture into a critically damaged one. Not only was he answerable to the owner but there was the broader ethical issue of removing early overpaint in the first place, for this could, after all, have been applied under Rembrandt's instruction. Bijl told me of spectral establishment figures who would attempt to "slaughter him" for even contemplating such a thing, branding him and his colleagues "money-makers and hunters of honor." These he had encountered all too often, and he knew that such critics rarely bothered to read detailed reports, preferring instead to listen "to their own noise." Had the painting been in good condition, he would not have countenanced the removal of the hair and hat, and nor indeed would Van de Wetering, even if they had been convinced that a fully authentic Rembrandt lay beneath.

"But this situation was not normal," Bijl stated emphatically. "We struggled for months with the problem. But all the time, however we considered it, there seemed to be only one way: straight forward. There were no remains of the hat, extended hair, or the earrings, and therefore nothing I could restore back. I could not have totally reconstructed them either, as the black-and-white photos were insufficient to work from, and anyway that would have been unethical too. Leaving the picture in its present state also felt unethical, given that as a caricature it would never be taken seriously and would quite possibly return to anonymity despite its qualities."

His arguments exhaustively considered and rehearsed, his position ring-fenced with moral reflection, but also deeply mindful of professional hazards, Bijl unwrapped his blades, mixed his solvents, took a deep breath and began by addressing the eye. What concerned him most was that the eye had been painted mainly in strong lead white, a notoriously hard and impenetrable pigment that had also defied the X-ray. He likened the initial prospect to surgically removing a tattoo from a face without damaging skin tissue.

During an investigative process that took many weeks, he began by creating with the point of a scalpel a tiny bore hole in the top-left corner of the eye socket, just large enough so that under microscopic analysis he could glimpse the layer beneath. The procedure was harrowing, requiring minute control and precision, but in the end he struck gold. He revealed a dark and complex pigment that proved to him, in that area at least, the existence of something authentic and preserved. Encouraged, but admitting that the trauma he risked causing to the picture sent a hot, sweaty feeling all through his body, he proceeded to do the same to the three other corners of the socket. Each revealed, in a similar way, a shadowy area of pigment. The prognosis was improving. More enthrallingly, when he compared each revealed area he noticed that the pigments slightly varied in tone and consistency, suggesting some sort of graded treatment.

He cautiously advanced by widening the bore holes to a millimeter in diameter to create what he described as "peep-holes." I now fully understood what the professor meant when he said that Bijl had guts. Bijl's excitement could still be felt as he recalled what these revealed: "Each opening exposed a slightly different tone of this dark underlying paint from which we could draw the conclusion that there was a complete, well-preserved, and modulated area beneath—in other words an eye in shadow!"

Emboldened, Bijl created connecting canals between each peephole. These further affirmed the existence of a well-preserved eye beneath: no technical, human or ethical constraint now harnessed him from taking his discovery to its conclusion. Having removed all the main overpaint around the eye, he embarked on the Sisyphean task of picking out the remnants in the grooves left by the hairs of the original brush. His work was now totally dependent on a microscope. He had to use more than five hundred scalpel blades, because after just a few applications each blade would lose its sharpness. The exotic added costume called for a different approach, first the use of solvents, then blades, a time-consuming procedure that gradually stripped away the later garments to reveal another form.

Bijl could almost feel the eyes of the art world looking over his shoulder, but there were other interested parties who were more directly preoccupied with the outcome of the painstaking operation. In the interests of scholarship Professor van de Wetering and the rest of the RRP committee were watching, but George Gordon from Sotheby's in London also made a number of visits to Alkmaar to chart the progress of what could ultimately become an important business proposition. Nicolas Joly of Sotheby's Paris, as the link with the owner, was in regular contact by telephone. He would then diligently report back to a lady who was by now naturally most interested in how her father's bequest was developing, particularly as the good news started flowing from the Netherlands that there was something exciting beneath the added layers of paint. She had said that she was in no particular hurry, but the auction house meanwhile waited in a state of heart-stopping anticipation for the "good surprise" that she had promised would trigger her decision to consign it to them for sale.

Throughout the process the restorer remained totally absorbed in what he was revealing, for it would benefit not only his clients but also the cause of Rembrandt scholarship. He liaised frequently with the professor, particularly when his archaeological penetration of the picture's depths exposed anything of consequence. It was during the latter stages of paint removal that he unearthed a compelling technical confirmation of his colleague's hypothesis. He managed to deduce that whoever had overpainted the picture in the seventeenth century had scratched a line in the hair with a sharp point, copying a technique Rembrandt himself often employed to add surface texture and animation to such areas. In so doing, that person had scored through to the layer beneath, which bore the indent in such a way as to reveal that the paint in that area had not dried. This neatly validated the professor's belief that the studio would update such paintings for the market relatively soon after their completion, probably two to three years after they had failed to sell—not long enough for some of Rembrandt's darker pigments fully to dry.

The whole restoration process took two years. This would be an inordinately long time for an unproblematic picture—most such works are cleaned and restored within a few days—but in this case it was entirely warranted. In characteristic fashion Van de Wetering conferred, argued about, weighed up and pondered all the painting's traits and attributes as they emerged. He was later to publish details of these ruminations, summing up his tortuously considered arguments with the portentous words "the conclusion reached . . . is that we are dealing with an autograph (i.e., fully authentic) work by Rembrandt. In July 2003 the owner kept her promise. I, together with hordes of others from the nether regions of the art world and beyond, came to the Sotheby's old-master preview on Bond Street to pay tribute to the rebirth of a hitherto entirely unknown painting.

The image Bijl had uncovered was little short of miraculous. Replete with characteristic moody shadowing, a more conservative fur-trimmed gown in place of the exotic paraphernalia and a penetrating look of intensity, it had mutated from an awkward hybrid into an original Rembrandt—the master himself inspecting his reflection in a mirror and recording it, as he did so often in a tireless voyage of introspection that lasted four decades.

When the auction opened, at midmorning on July 10, it was standing room only in a salesroom densely packed with the trade, private buyers, onlookers, television crews, journalists and Sotheby's staff on telephones.

For one man, however—who was at the sale in all but person—it was 5:30 A.M. According to George Gordon, who was in contact with him, he had taken his telephone into the bathroom so as not to wake his wife. Steve Wynn, the Las Vegas gambling and hotel colossus, was already well known to Sotheby's, and indeed the rest of the art world, for his prominent collection of paintings that mainly straddled the late nineteenth and twentieth centuries, beginning with the Impressionists and concluding with Andy Warhol. They were on show in the headquarters of his casino operation, where visitors were given the opportunity to be led around with an audio guide recorded by Wynn himself. Given his interest in what he saw as key moments in the history of art, a Rembrandt self-portrait offered the perfect justification to leap into the seventeenth century with a particularly spectacular splash.

Sotheby's had estimated that the picture would sell for in excess of £5 million. In today's market this would be considered cheap, but there were others around, myself included, who were aware of its having been overpainted, and this modification subsequently removed, however expertly, may have diminished the original impact a little. Even with the attentions of a superb restorer, a painting that had been ministered to as much as this was bound to show a degree of postoperative trauma. As it transpired, the bidding was brisk, and out of earshot of his sleeping wife, Wynn managed to secure the painting against an unknown telephone bidder for a total, including commission, of just under £7 million. Had this picture reached the market without all its subsequent inquiries, attentions and restoration, looking as strange as it had done, it could quite easily have turned up in a minor sale valued at just a few thousand dollars.

For Bijl the picture's recovery was not only a vindication of van de Wetering's hypothesis that this was an autographed original, which, failing to find a buyer, his assistants had exotically refashioned—but another hugely valuable experience of the workings of an artist he adored. Another emotion was readable in the grin across his face, a look that had replaced the angst of seeking to convey the technical feats and academic challenges he had faced. Having finished his exhausting travelogue through the picture's restorations, he briefly mused on the risks he had taken, concluding with boyish directness: "Privately I have always wanted to be one of the best, to be highly respected. I know this when I play football: I'm a bad loser."

"What would your father think of you now?" I could not resist asking.

"At the end of his life he appeared to be proud of me. I only know that because my mother told me. But it's not for him I do this—it's my internal motor that drives me," he said.

As he smiled broadly and tilted back in his chair, I picked up the same ironic indomitability I had noticed in Ernst van de Wetering. It was difficult to put my finger on exactly where it came from. Success was part of it, the feeling of being part of a top team was clearly in there, and so too was the acclaim and regard they enjoyed. But about both men there was also a degree of self-awareness that diluted their pride. They knew they were far from being Rembrandt. They had devoted large portions of their lives to understanding one of the greatest artists in the world, and yet ultimately they accepted their limitations. They were wise enough and war-weary enough after years of academic struggles to know that attribution relies on the power of argument and that although they had advanced the field with extraordinary clarity and insight, Rembrandt himself would never be around to give them a reassuring thumbs up.

"Oh, and there is another aspect to this when I consider it," Bijl added as if surprising himself with a sudden realization. "Doing what I do can be such fun as well; you really have no idea."

Despite the rigorous demands of scholarship and the stringent risks, they were partly motivated by the thrill of the chase—something to which I could instantly relate. This very human impulse is as essential to scholarship and academia as it is to dealing, providing a zest that fuels the pace of discovery and revelation. At an unspecified date around May 2008 Steve Wynn sold the Page self-portrait via Otto Naumann. It was bought, perhaps needless to say, by Tom Kaplan.

CHAPTER 5

A Queen in Distress

There is a lot of fulfillment to art dealing: the investigation that leads in an unforeseen direction, the revelation when a hunch is confirmed, the first moment of re-presentation, the vindication of risk when a sale is completed. In my own specialization there is also a delightful added kick that comes from focusing on portraits of significance when they make their way into the arms of a historical institution. To stand back and watch your rehatched item being deemed, not just by yourself but also by the art establishment, to be something of enduring importance provides that warm feeling of a job well done, giving added reason for choosing a life devoted to dealing in secondhand goods.

It was in a downstairs room at Hever, the childhood home of Anne Boleyn, the second of Henry VIII's hapless queens, that a particularly memorable historical coming together first took place. All of us around the breakfast table had arrived at the castle the night before. Scenically positioned in the rural Weald of Kent, Hever Castle reascended to prominence in 1903 when it was bought and lovingly restored by the statesman and financier William Waldorf Astor (great-grandson of John Jacob Astor, said in his day to be the first millionaire in America), who affirmed his affection for England by adopting British nationality. His desire for security and secrecy was such that he never let guests stay at the castle itself, seeking refuge with his family behind the moat and drawbridge. Astor's descendants sold Hever in 1983 to a Yorkshire-based company called Broadland Properties Ltd., who radically reversed the trend by professionally opening it to the public; John Guthrie, the company's chairman, his wife, Faith, and their daughter and two sons were our hosts that morning.

Bob Pullin, Hever's manager, had been a crucial figure in the castle's changed function. A fit and well-groomed golfing enthusiast in his early sixties, Bob had at one time been Lord Mountbatten's house manager and before that a schoolteacher. With flair and a punctilious desire to communicate history, he had taken great strides, with Guthrie's support, to bring back to the castle a whiff of Tudor England, including building up a collection of early portraits of national stature for the edification of the 300,000 who visit the castle each year. The latest and most important recent acquisition, a portrait of Arthur, Prince of Wales, Henry VIII's brother, was to be unveiled that morning. I had been invited to attend as the man who had sold the picture to them.

As television, radio and newspaper journalists gathered in one of the castle's upstairs rooms, Bob was pacing. Although around the table was nearly the full complement from the night before, including Sir Timothy Clifford, the recently retired director of the museums of Scotland, and the eminent business-man Sir Angus Grossheart, there was no sign of David Starkey, the man whom the press had come to watch perform. Starkey's partner, James Brown, had begun by explaining to those around him how a freak east wind running down the ancient chimney breast of their bedroom had howled all night. Sleep had thus largely eluded them. Bob was now contemplating the gloomy prospect of his star attraction being either well and truly exhausted or, worse still, fast asleep.

The picture that was creating a stir that morning was in some ways the most important I had ever had the good fortune to discover, although the revelation had happened close to a decade earlier. Arthur, Prince of Wales, died at the age of fif-teen shortly after marrying his Spanish bride, Catherine of Aragon. Although not a historical heavyweight like his brother, Henry, he was nonetheless the first heir to the Tudor throne, and the implications of his premature death for English history were substantial, not least because Henry then married Arthur's widow to safeguard the diplomatic advantages that she brought. The rest is a familiar tale. Henry's subsequent divorce from Catherine to marry Anne Boleyn led to the Reformation and England's break with Rome, changing the nation's religious orientation and character forever.

I had discovered the portrait at a London auction house, where it had fallen under the hammer as a rather different-looking work. At some point in the past four centuries someone had decided to turn it into a larger painting by adding side panels, usefully (from my point of view) disguising its diminu-tive original appearance. What made the picture preeminent was that we had been able to prove—having removed the later additions and the copious overpaint—that this portably small panel, originally from the Royal Collection, was the only contemporary portrait of Arthur and was probably painted for his marriage negotiations at the end of the fifteenth century. Miraculously it had survived the vicissitudes of history and changing ownership, and although I had sold it nine years earlier (buying my London town house with the proceeds) I had recently managed to buy it back from the owner and then sell it on to Hever. This was deeply satisfying, for now I knew it could be assured both a public and—given that this was the childhood home of Arthur's doomed sister-in-law—a historically apposite setting where it could function with meaning. David Starkey had been invited to unveil the prince.

To the British documentary-watching public, Starkey's is a face as familiar as that of Henry VIII, a historian whose reputation has been forged through constant broadcasting and some twenty books (he is a fellow of Cambridge University and a specialist in, among other things, the social etiquette of Henry's household). Over the years he has developed a seductive delivery style that oscillates between pulpit thumping and backstairs gossip. Delighting in controversy, if not deliberately seeking it, he moves seamlessly from the nuances of the British constitution to the vicissitudes of human inclinations. The prospect of anointing Arthur at his new seat had appealed to Starkey, not least because some years earlier he had engaged in the analysis of an unknown portrait, which he convincingly proved to be none other than Henry's fifth queen, Catherine Howard, and he understood the inestimable value of putting faces to history.

With ten minutes to go before the press briefing, to the

conspicuous relief of those gathered, Starkey entered the breakfast room through the Gothic door leading from the bedrooms. A compact, neatly built man with sharply adversarial eyes, horn-rimmed glasses and a faultlessly cut suit, he possessed all the presence of a well-known character actor, but that morning as he entered the castle's breakfast room, his head slightly bowed he had the bleary look of a lesser mortal.

"I suppose at least the wind was an authentic Tudor experience," he said wearily as his cooked breakfast was placed before him.

Although he had taken the seat next to me, apart from brief pleasantries I left him undisturbed until I noticed the angle of his head lift and his eyes flicker with signs of life. Bob, who was deeply heartened that his guest was at least upright, now restlessly hovered, waiting to escort him away. I decided to test the waters.

"Do you know what you're going to say?" I asked. Starkey had by now drained his coffee and pigmentation was returning to his cheeks.

"Oh, just the normal old stuff," he responded with a wolfish smile. The performer inside had also clambered out of bed, and was readying himself for his public.

I have attended many unveilings of paintings, both contemporary and historical. They follow a fairly standard pattern: introductory speech of welcome; address by the guest of honor (or sometimes by the subject of the painting); ceremonial lifting of the veil; murmurs of polite approval; and then the publicity shots of the individuals next to the work. These events normally take place in large public rooms, but Bob had wanted to give the press a more sensuous sixteenth-century experience. The castle's cabinet room, where Arthur was to be hung in the company of other Tudor royals, is markedly small and intimate, as well as dark, and as we all walked up the narrow staircase, past William Astor's meticulously refurbished paneling, much of it bedecked with tapestries and portraits, I noticed that a number of people had decided to wait outside in the light. I found room to stand near the door, from where I could observe the expressions of the fifteen or so photographers, journalists and cameramen, as well as the assembly of some twenty guests.

John Guthrie said a few words about the collection, introduced Starkey and stood aside to allow him to draw back the curtain. There was a cacophony of clicks as the cameras captured the unveiler and the unveiled. It felt distinctly odd to see the small portrait, the repository of so much emotion and sense of risk nine years earlier, now on its own. People often ask whether it is difficult to let go of pictures, and the answer is that the art dealer can feel like a redundant midwife on these occasions. But, seeing Arthur up there in his gold robe and emerald green background in the context of his extended family (the castle's collection includes portraits of Henry and all his wives and children), I drew comfort from the fact that he was now functioning as his maker—in this case an anonymous artist—had intended.

Starkey's familiar donnish diction soon seized our attention. As he turned to the portrait I had a clammy fear that he would say something waspish—he has been known to give no quarter to pictures that don't pass muster—but I was spared. Arthur, he proposed, was a strong and lusty young lad by contemporary account, far from being the sickly child Catherine claimed had been unable to consummate his marriage. He then went on to cite the contemporary herald who testified that the couple had made love on their wedding night. Having dealt with the close-ups, he panned out to give us wide shots of Henry VII (Arthur's father) galloping through the woods to gain a sneak preview of his son's bride and the lavish arrangements for the power wedding. Within the first few minutes not only had he brought in sex and provided cinematic color, but he had challenged his audience with a historical contention: sleeping with a brother's "consummated" widow was defined as incest by a strict application of the Bible, proving that his brother was not up to fulfilling his marital obligations was thus of paramount importance to Henry, a king scrabbling around for justifications to divorce his consort following her failure to produce a male heir (and given his growing ardor for Anne Boleyn). The "did he or didn't he" argument over Arthur's priapic powers still consumed historians, and Starkey was adding his view, bolstered with contemporary evidence. By the end of his address this late fifteenth-century oil-on-panel portrait had mutated into a pulsating teenager, heaving under the weight of dynastic expectation. I left the room convinced that Arthur was well and truly launched and that I could now leave him to fend for himself.

The unveiling was to be followed by a small reception, and as I made my way downstairs I overheard a journalist discussing with one of the castle guides what he had just learned. "Why didn't I have a guy like that teaching me history at school?" he lamented. "My life could have been so different!"

Starkey has played an important role in several instances in reidentifying lost faces using primary historical research. The first to do this in a dramatic way was Susan James, who debunked a portrait that had been hanging for thirty years at the National Portrait Gallery. I recall reading about the picture with astonishment. It was thought to represent Lady Jane Grey, the teenage claimant to the English throne following the death of her cousin, Edward VI—a brief flirtation with royalty that ended with her execution. By carefully studying the surviving inventories of Tudor jewels and comparing them with those that the sitter was wearing in the painting, James managed conclusively to prove that the National Portrait Gallery's picture couldn't be the ill-fated "nine-day queen"—she was wearing the wrong jewels. A portrait that had become the schoolbook image of Lady Jane was instead proved to be of Henry's VIII's sixth and last wife, Catherine Parr. The label was duly changed.

In 2003 Starkey tackled a miniature portrait of an unknown lady with the same forensic rigor. It belonged to the Royal Collection and was acknowledged to be by Hans Holbein, the great Northern master who settled in London during the reign of Henry VIII. Starkey had a hunch that it represented the flirtatious and unfaithful Catherine Howard, for which proclivities Henry had her beheaded. She certainly had an errant look about her—the knowing quarter smile placed it among Holbein's most suggestive characterizations—but as no other image of her was known for comparison, it needed proof. Here Starkey had an advantage. What she was wearing was portrayed in brilliantly readable detail—Holbein was also a jewelry designer and knew his way around stones and their elaborate settings—and Starkey had just been studying the inventory of Catherine's jewels, a detailed list compiled by the clerk of the king's wardrobe, Nicholas Bristowe. A besotted Henry had lavished beads, pendants and stones on his beautiful young bride: some had belonged to her deceased predecessor, Queen Jane Seymour, and inconveniently included her initials, but the majority were more up-to-date, exquisitely wrought and highly valuable tokens of his esteem, power jewelry intended to ensure that no other outshone his chosen one.

Starkey got to work scrutinizing the descriptions line by line and testing them against the miniature. He did not have to spend long at this, for he found that the first of the listed items—a carefully described gold headdress with diamonds, rubies and pearls—was the very one she was wearing. On her shapely bosom which was covered by a translucent chemise, hung a most elaborate and chunky necklace, and again it matched precisely another described in the inventory: idiosyncratic clusters of four pearls interspersed with twenty-four rubies. To round off the identification, there was a description of the pendant hanging from the necklace, made up of a "fair table diamond" and a "very fair Ruby." There could be little doubt: an anonymous face had been transformed into a recognizable queen and history given a new visage. The irony was that in its early history the painting had been called *Queen Catherine Howard* but had subsequently been demoted, for no particular reason, and it took Starkey's simple piece of forensic proof to reestablish it.

Over drinks an hour later I suggested that there might be opportunities for consulting with him in the future—he with his desire to illuminate history and we with our pursuit of lost faces. His response was guardedly encouraging. If anything interesting emerged, he suggested, I should let him know.

In late 2006 we decided to hold an exhibition of our discoveries in Tudor art and to widen it into a general overview of the subject. Given that Starkey had guest-curated for others, most notably an exhibition on Elizabeth I at the National Maritime Museum, I asked him whether he would like to do so for us—and to include some examples of his own. He and his partner, James Brown, a publisher and, among other things, specialist on Tudor badges, rose to the challenge with vigor, and over the course of a year we put together a significant show, with a catalogue edited by my researcher Bendor Grosvenor, entitled *Lost Faces*.

There are some events that can be described as quantum leaps in the history of a business, and this was certainly one: the public poured into our gallery—more than two thousand visitors in all—and although some were disappointed not to meet Starkey himself, the Tudor queens and sovereigns amply compensated. A number of leading international collections lent us their works and one portrait in particular, a miniature of a hitherto unknown lady on loan from the Yale Center for British Art, in New Haven, Connecticut, became a star turn. Starkey ingeniously argued, with the assistance of Bendor, that it could represent Lady Jane Grey, on the basis of floral emblems, jewelry and birth date. Since the great debunking by Susan James there had been only one new contender: an out-of-period copy bought by the National Portrait Gallery from a London dealer, a picture that Starkey had mercilessly laid into, stating the grounds for identification to be flimsy and unconvincing. Having waited for his moment, the affronted dealer launched, in the *Antiques Trade Gazette* shortly after our exhibition, a bilious attack on Starkey's championing of the new Lady Jane Grey. Amply rebuffed by Starkey, the harangue added an amusing diversion to what was an extraordinary two-week enterprise during which we proposed new identities for portraits of two other wives of Henry VIII, Anne Boleyn and Catherine Howard. The exhibition has helped stimulate interest in an area that has been bedeviled by iconographic confusion. In holding it I got to know Starkey's working techniques, and the friendship that followed has led to further collaborative advances, one of which took place as I was writing this book.

Bendor's driving ambition, apart from fulfilling his role and duties as a director of the company, is to find and discover lost works of art of historical significance. He is an irritatingly accomplished combination of distinguished historian and fast-developing connoisseur who can recognize signature strokes and condition better than most people I know. Whenever he alerts me to a picture he has found in some distant location I look carefully. The one he dropped in front of me one morning was closer to home, however, in the form of a large color illustration in the Sotheby's preview magazine highlighting forthcoming attractions. A man who does not articulate his emotion demonstratively and is highly economical with his words, Bendor often uses no more than insinuation and body language to convey intent. I have seen him use this laconic form of expression to great effect on gallery suppliers who fall short of the mark.

"This is something we need to consider," he said quietly, folding back the page and placing it before me.

The illustration was of a full-length portrait of Elizabeth I that was to go under the hammer in a couple of months' time. At first glance it was easy to see why he was captivated. Not only are full-length contemporary portraits of the Virgin Queen inordinately rare, but this appeared to be the earliest. By tradition it had been presented by Elizabeth to Griffin Hampden, sheriff of Buckingham, with whom she was staying at his fine mansion on one of her royal processions. Richly attired in a red dress with puffing white slashes, and festooned with pearls and embroidered X-shaped crosses, she was both spectacular and otherworldly. In her hand she held a gillyflower, or wild carnation, a traditional symbol of betrothal. She stood before a highly ornate gold cloth of state, her hand resting on the cushion of a throne, and beside it was a thicket of fruits, flowers, and vegetables, clearly intended to impart meaning. She also appeared oddly unassimilated with her background: her hand seemed not to connect properly with the throne, while her bell-shaped dress and hips were silhouetted to give the appearance of an ornamental figurine.

Portraits of Elizabeth are the ultimate trophy to collectors, museums and enthusiasts of the period. Although desirable as the records of a famous sovereign, they are also testaments to a semimystical cult surrounding an extraordinary woman who dared to command a stage generally restricted to men. About 160 are recorded from her lifetime—many in a poor state of preservation—commissioned and sometimes given to those who wished to express a loyalty and association with the crown, as well as for diplomatic purposes. They reveal her as empress, figurehead, goddess and heroine, providing a window into her times. Sometimes they are suffused with complex symbols relating to wisdom, virginity and power. On a deeper level they consoled a population starved for religious art following the Reformation: she was the nation's Virgin Mary, stripped of her halo and reconditioned with the trappings of earthly wealth and power. As she got older, and her resolve not to marry grew more obvious, her image evolves into Gloriana, a desexed and almost abstract figure embodying and guiding the nation's fortunes. Today it is not just those susceptible to the intrigue and aesthetics of the later Tudor court, or the literary world of Spenser and Shakespeare, who are drawn to these icons, but a broader art-buying public enthralled by their impact, and including on one occasion a collector of Andy Warhol pictures. In my career as a dealer I have handled or owned six prime examples, and each has been a high point.

One in particular remained in my thinking that morning. It had appeared two years earlier at a sale at Christie's South Kensington and was described as a copy of the famous portrait of Elizabeth in the Royal Collection—the-Queen-to-be as a precocious, scholarly thirteen-year-old in a radiant crimson dress beside a learned book. It had an estimate of £6,000–£8,000. During much of that time Elizabeth lived a life of uncertainty and fear, a feral existence in which she relied on her wits to repulse the accusations of inquisitors that she was plotting to take the throne from her half-sister, Mary. Given the fate of her mother, Anne Boleyn, portraits of the marginalized bastard princess were thus not in demand at that stage of her life. No certainly known contemporary painting (other than in group portraits as a child) of Elizabeth as a princess was known to exist apart from the one in the Royal Collection.

I had taken a taxi to Christie's in a less than optimistic mood, for the chances of the picture being original were remote, and I felt no more upbeat when I laid eyes on her among the other offerings on the wall. Vast quantities of overpaint clouded her head, hands and dress. I also noticed the later addition of two side panels (the work was painted on oak panel), replacing ones that had probably existed originally.

However, the longer I stayed with her and the more I looked, the more I gained promising glimpses of another form. There were a few passages that the relentless later paint had failed to cover, particularly in the fingers, where I could detect a reassuringly granular, marble-like finish. It is here that art dealing gets closest to archaeology, putting me in mind of how hidden remains can be rerevealed as a result of surface clues. Although I did not anticipate the emergence of a slice of lost civilization, I was nonetheless excited by the picture's possibilities and therefore very pleased when it was knocked down to me for £43,000, an entirely manageable sum for a speculation with a potentially very exciting upside.

Later that week, under the restorer's ruthless lights, it was possible to diagnose not one but two layers, or campaigns, of overpaint. The upper, much of it on her face, was relatively easy to remove. It was clear that it had been applied in the past one hundred years, and the process of removing it was like scraping jam from a piece of bread. The lower layer was more tricky and required the insistent use of solvents and scalpels to pick away and dissolve encrusted pigment that could have been as much as two centuries old. After the side panels had been removed and the losses touched in, an arrestingly beautiful image emerged with the honest look of a contemporary portrait—the solemn princess impressing the viewer with her evidently fine mind, her body and her famously elegant hands. The overpaint had most probably been added to cover up localized damage as well as the join marks of the added panels, and might well have been done in the face to pretty her up—in a bizarrely inappropriate manner.

Dendrochronology proved that the Baltic oak that supplied

the panel could have been felled as early as 1546. This finding supported a dating that we had arrived at anyway, partly on grounds of technique but also because Elizabeth as a princess would have been a most unsuitable image to circulate after her succession to the throne.

What added to the picture's status was that we had managed to determine from a Christie's inventory number on the reverse (historically applied to all pictures the auction house has sold or considered since the nineteenth century) that in the early twentieth century it had been owned by a direct descendant of the Duke of Somerset, a family known to the princess, not least through Protector Somerset during the reign of Edward VI. Subsequently it had been acquired by Spanish collectors who, we later deduced, were the last owners.

With great fanfare we exhibited the picture for the first time at the Grosvenor House Art and Antiques Fair in London, considerably increasing the footfall to the annual event following its prominent coverage on television and in national newspapers. In three days we had sold it.

Although the memory of this revelation was still fresh in our minds, the painting that Bendor was now recommending to me was a very different proposition. For a start it had an estimate of between £700,000 and £1 million. It had been marketed across the world through Sotheby's magazine. From the illustration it seemed that overpaint was minimal, although subsequently we radically revised this view. The portrait also had the huge advantage of a firm attribution to a known artist, Steven van der Meulen, initially proposed by the art historian Sir Roy Strong after close comparison with two other works believed to be by the same hand. Described in his day as "the famous paynter Steven," Van der Meulen settled in London in 1560 and was subsequently perceived by art historians as the most important court painter of the early 1560s. To round it off, Sotheby's had made an impressive attempt to establish its purpose and function.

Speculating that the Queen had most likely had herself painted as an advertisement for marriage, Sotheby's drew attention to her youth and the profusion of flowers and fruit. They latched onto an important figure among the earlier suitors, Erik XIV of Sweden, whose portrait attributed to Van der Meulen is believed to have been presented by one of Erik's marriage envoys to the Queen in 1561. Could this have been painted as the return offering? They also listed other contenders who, like Erik, failed to make the matrimonial grade, such as Archdukes Ferdinand and Charles of Austria. These two were favored by William Cecil, Elizabeth's adviser, but their resistance to converting from Catholicism ruled them out in the Queen's eyes. They also proposed, very plausibly, that the portrait could be related to a proclamation of 1563, preserved as a draft in the state papers, intended to prevent unflattering images of the Queen. The proclamation effectively sought a painter with sensitivity and public-relations skills to project in paint what could not always be put into words. Although imposing, she was not a conventionally beautiful woman, having her father's small mouth and hawklike nose, and she is known to have smashed images of herself she did not like into pieces and hurled them into a fire. There was also the more ethereal, symbolic resonance she sought in her depiction.

It did not need much imagination or scholarship to understand that what was being offered could be of unprecedented importance: a seminal full-length portrait of a monarch more identified with the history of Britain than any other—a hugely elaborate piece of statecraft with all the impact of theater, the significance of a state paper and a sovereign human presence. Given that the work fell squarely into our area as dealers we had no option but to look at it very seriously. And yes, from the illustration and description, it also looked relatively cheap.

Bendor and I walked up the road to Sotheby's. Although it was a month before public sale viewing, the salesroom had accommodated us by offering an informal preview, as all the main rooms do for serious potential buyers who express enthusiasm. After making our way along a series of corridors, down steep staircases and through security-coded doors, we found the picture propped up on blocks in the auction room's basement, a cavernous, subterranean storeroom stacked high with innumerable framed canvases destined for forthcoming sales, surrounded by worktops piled with books and papers relating to work in progress.

On the floor next to the portrait was a high-powered flashlight plugged into the main circuit. The catalogue assistant, a fresh-faced internee in his early twenties, looked on as I moved forward to scrutinize the surface of the dress, using the flashlight to illuminate detail. At the level I was looking, from above the Queen's waist down to her groin, my gaze hit a wall of shocking disappointment. Oceans of overpaint covered almost everything before me. Many of the X-shaped embroidered crosses I had seen in the photograph and which so distinguished the design of the fabric consisted of no more than perfunctory scribbles on a coating of disingenuous red. Overpaint on a sixteenth-century painting has a soupish, coagulated appearance, in contrast to the mineral-rich, cracked surface of the real thing; the poor woman was covered by the stuff.

Standing back, I looked at the image as a whole and noticed that, rather than the marble-like texture I was seeking, the surface had a dull, waxy smoothness that seemed ascribable to the transfer process and the leaching through of underlying wax or glue. I knew that the picture had been transferred from panel to canvas because it had said so in the Sotheby's write-up, and now it all made sense. The picture had been deadened. The perilous business of transferral to canvas, gladly no longer practiced, was much favored by the Hermitage Museum in St. Petersburg in the first half of the twentieth century, and the fashion spread. Instead of attempting to stabilize a panel picture whose planks had worked loose or were partially rotted—common afflictions in early British portraits—conservators would sometimes plane down the reverse of the oak panel till it was paper thin and then apply it to canvas. Not only did the adhesives sometimes adversely affect the texture of the paint surface, but during this hazardous act of carpentry the plane could sometimes tear through to the surface, causing irreparable loss and the need for copious repair and patch-up.

I indicated to Bendor that it was not what it should be, but he had started looking at the portrait at his eye level, eight inches higher than mine and was more occupied with what was going on at her cleavage. By this stage I had all but written it off, but he was keen to point out that where he was looking there were some very fine passages in the jewelry and face. To my shame, however, the doors were shutting, my interest terminating, and

I asked to see another picture that was on offer, a portrait by Joshua Reynolds of the eighteenth-century beauty Kitty Fisher. Trying to salvage portraits that have largely perished is often a grim and thankless business, tantamount to giving CPR to a cold corpse, and I just didn't have the enthusiasm. I had also now twigged why the estimate was so low. A portrait like this in fine condition would be worth millions, a picture that would fly at auction, chased by bidders from both sides of the Atlantic, particularly if one could convincingly unwrap its history. Its dismal physical predicament had effectively grounded it.

Bendor continued to mention the portrait from time to time over the next few weeks, for it had never quite left his mind, but I had largely forgotten it by the time we went to view the entire sale on the first public viewing day. It was then that something unexpected happened. I thought I was beyond being impressed by the skills of mere presentation, but I will admit that she looked rather different. Hanging on a large wall, evenly lit, a carpet beneath her, it was as if her time in the basement had been one of confinement and she had now ascended to her public function. There was no doubt that even with the swaths of overpaint she retained the bones of an affecting royal presence. When considering a painting at auction one of the many tests to which you put it is to imagine how it will look in your gallery and what sort of impact it may have on your colleagues, friends and, above all, clients when they see it there. A telling foretaste of this can be gained by watching how the public respond to it at the auction preview. Even though that morning the preview was sparsely attended, there was hardly a moment when someone was not standing before the picture, waylaid by its monumental presence and drawn to discover more by reading its label. I began to question my initial response, mindful also that Bendor had never quite let it go. In a low whisper we discussed it further and I ended with the suggestion that she deserved a second look—this time with an ultraviolet lamp that might show up some or all the overpaint. He was off sorting it before I had finished the sentence.

Leading off the main viewing room is a small, cell-like space without windows, which, with the overhead light turned off, provides complete darkness. Two porters unhooked the (six-feet-six-inch-high) canvas from the wall and for the second time we now came face-to-face with it in unprepossessing surroundings, subjecting it to the type of scrutiny that its subject herself had endured while a princess. It had struck me as ironically comparable: our purpose was not very different from that of those who had imprisoned the twenty-year-old Elizabeth in the Tower of London and sought to discover the truth behind her reported actions and words. She probably *had* been plotting to overthrow her Catholic sister Queen Mary, but her brilliant advocacy both concealed and outwitted attempts to prove it. If we were going to establish the truth beneath the sham, and consider paying the sort of money that was being suggested, our own inquisition needed to be ruthlessly incisive.

A retired American radiologist who was viewing the sale and had seen the portrait being manhandled into the tiny room asked whether he could join us, pointing out that this was the type of scientific analysis and diagnosis he had done all his life, but on people. Quite why he used a UV lamp on his patients might have explained his retirement, but as he appeared anything other than a prospective bidder, I was happy for him to join us. Thus, as we were plunged into darkness, it felt rather like a cramped séance as the blue light flickered on, the radiologist (his wife had remained outside as she disliked small spaces) standing behind and breathing rather heavily, Sotheby's specialist in British paintings Emmeline Hallmark on my left, Bendor on my right, and the Queen's luminescent body and face taking form under the lamp's strengthening beam.

The first area I homed in on was the one I had first seen in the basement, around her waist and lower skirt, and the result was predictable: it fluoresced bright purple, revealing an area not unlike the shape of the Atlantic and about eighteen inches square. Moving the lamp above and below this area revealed similar but smaller passages of overpaint, and it began to become clear that they loosely equated to where the panels had obviously once split, a notorious cause of paint loss, and that the conservator had spaded on huge quantities of pigment to conceal the repair work around the joins. The face had even more conspicuously fluorescing dabs and flecks, but these, Emmeline pointed out, were work they had recently commissioned from a restorer to rectify some distracting blemishes for the sale.

I handed the lamp to Bendor, who carefully studied the jewelry around her neck and cleavage, noting another large area of daubed-on later paint on her right shoulder, before moving to the throne and the gold cloth of state. This was more tricky because of the way the shell gold (an early form of applied gold that takes its name from the mussel shells used to store it) deflected the beam, but it appeared that much of the design had been strengthened in a later hand too, large areas of the metal either lost or covered. He passed the lamp back and I cast its light onto the backdrop of vegetation. In radical contrast to the other troubled passages it appeared pristinely free of later paint. Apart from minor sprinkled infills, the fruits, flowers and peas retained the fresh, lush physical presence of produce harvested that morning. Their contrasting state of high preservation was both striking and uplifting. It also got me thinking. Could the rest of the picture have been similarly spared but unnecessarily smeared over? If, just if, the areas of overpaint were clumsily excessive, and the paint layer beneath largely intact, there was hope.

"So what can you see, and what's the diagnosis?" asked the radiologist, who, apart from his noisy inhalations, had all this time retained a professional silence.

"A queen in distress—with an uncertain prognosis," I replied. He seemed unexpectedly satisfied with that flippant answer and we then piled out of the dark hole, he to his waiting wife and we to the gallery for further reflection.

Bendor normally tells me straight if I have overlooked something he considers to be of importance. This time, given my lack of delectation for the portrait in the first place, he was more subtle. He e-mailed me, which, considering that my office is barely ten paces from his, carried a certain weight. I had till that point been more interested in the Reynolds of Kitty Fisher, a swift, poetic, unfinished sketch of a seductive courtesan, but the Queen's emerging allure was fast displacing these affections. Given that the Reynolds was estimated at £1–£2 million, it had to be one or the other. Registering my growing enthusiasm, Bendor acknowledged it and added, "I find the prospect of Elizabeth more enticing." It was his courteous way of telling me that—finally—I was doing what I was told.

I picked up the telephone and called Alfred Bader in

Milwaukee. In return for a percentage of the profit, Alfred had backed a number of my major purchases and had proved to be a trusting and solid business partner. If our inquiries into the picture's potential over the next three days were to prove positive, I was going to require the big guns, and so I needed to warm him up. I had mentioned the picture to him some weeks earlier, but had also told him I preferred the Reynolds. Now, rather awkwardly, I needed to switch his focus. I decided to sell it to him hard—I knew I could back out without a problem—and laid it on about how exciting it *could* be.

"What do you think it will cost?" came his immediate response, brushing aside my hyperbole.

"Over the estimate," I replied, although I had not given this calculation much thought.

"That's a lot of money"—his usual first response to almost everything I suggest.

"What about the condition?" he then asked.

"I shall have to get back to you," I replied.

"As you know, I have the funds. Let me know how you go."

He went on to tell me about a £300–£500 painting he had spotted in a sale in Sussex which involved as much, if not more, expenditure of brainpower than the £1 million–plus Elizabeth.

I felt in need of art history, or more particularly, history. Bendor had already put aside his other tasks and gone straight to the London Library, and I spoke to him that evening. Given that he had already been quietly harvesting and baling information over the previous weeks, all he needed, he told me, was a few more hours for a first hypothesis. It would be ready in the morning.

My next call was to Katherine Ara, a restorer known to

Alfred Bader with great experience in Tudor portraiture (I had also spotted her looking at the picture earlier at the auction house). I commissioned as thorough a diagnosis and prognosis as she was able to provide. I also told her I needed it as soon as possible. The request was simple even if the task was not: tell me if you can, I asked her, what lies beneath the later paint. The painting's monumentality and detail, combined with what I knew about the aesthetics of Tudor portraiture, were beginning to suggest to me that, although now hampered by overpaint, and possibly even irreparably damaged beneath, it was likely at one time to have been an image of almost superhuman impact. Ara's technical insights could get us a few degrees closer to the truth.

The next day, having marshaled his thoughts, Bendor was ready to deliver. His office desk was awash with articles and books. Sitting at his screen with a further book in his hand, his reading glasses latched to his nose, in characteristic sotto voce he incisively began the case for the prosecution. Every bit a modern historian, and not unlike Starkey, his approach is first to understand the playing field and the rules of engagement, and then to apply commonsense psychology. What had particularly interested him was a crucial series of events that befell Elizabeth four years into her reign, in 1562–63, a period of intrigue, insecurity and ambition as compelling as any fiction, with a febrile atmosphere, in which propaganda and artistic statement could readily generate.

When Elizabeth came to the throne, in 1558, the universal expectation was that she would marry. In the eyes of the time she was in dire need of male support financially, morally and physically. Not only was she a woman, but she had once been declared illegitimate and was now the last of the Tudor line. She rebuffed all approaches to marry with teasing evasion, but by 1563 matters had come to a head: she had narrowly avoided death from smallpox the previous year, not least because the medical advice she was given (a hot bath followed by a cold walk) was inept. With the court convinced she was about to die, she stunned them all by stating that Robert Dudley should be appointed Regent. Dudley, Master of the Horse, was the Queen's favorite and believed by many to have been her secret lover, manipulating his way into royal trust, and office, with a combination of aristocratic pedigree and sex appeal. Surviving portraits lucidly suggest the type of man Elizabeth had fallen for: a cosmopolitan, languid, beautifully attired ladykiller—possibly literally. Two years earlier Dudley's wife had been found dead with a broken neck, having fallen down the stairs of her house, and although cleared of any involvement he was widely thought to have murdered her. The son of an executed traitor (John Dudley, Duke of Northumberland, mastermind of Lady Jane Grey's brief reign), Dudley was viewed with deep concern and hostility by the rest of the court. Elizabeth's cousin Mary Queen of Scots summed up the prevailing perception with icy directness: "The Queen of England is going to marry her horsekeeper, who has killed his wife to make room for her."

Following her recovery the big question was, who would succeed the Queen if she died without child? By statute it was the younger sister of the executed Jane Grey, Katherine Grey, who suffered from debilitating anorexia. By blood it was Mary

Queen of Scots, a Catholic, and the country had only just recovered from Mary I's violent attempts to get the country to readopt the old religion. Henry VIII was briefly succeed by his son, Edward VI, who died six years later and was followed briefly by his cousin, the Protestant Lady Jane Grey. She was followed by Mary I, Henry's daughter by Catherine of Aragon. She remained a Catholic and sought to undo her father's Reformation. Elizabeth, who succeeded her, swung the pendulum back to Protestantism. To the Tudors the baffling choice of two unsuitable queens, for a country that should anyway be ruled by a man, was little short of terrifying, embodying the hideous prospect of returning to the civil wars of the previous century. The court and assembly therefore made renewed efforts to get Elizabeth to marry. In the meantime they requested that she name an heir, not least because there were rumors that she was now infertile following her illness. But although the House of Commons and the House of Lords sent petitions, she sidestepped their intent with sophistic evasion.

Surely, Bendor argued, a portrait of this magnitude must have something to do with this pivotal standoff? Yes, the image was laced with symbols of fertility and union appropriate to her sex and broader destiny. But for a highly sophisticated woman, steeped in scholarship and guile, there had to be a lurking Shakespearean subplot. Although the idea of a marriage portrait could not be ruled out, Elizabeth had bigger fish to fry—namely her own independence, sovereignty and desire not to be shoehorned into a constitutional solution.

"There is something else you should be aware of," Bendor added with the suggestion of a smile after we had finished our ruminations on the historical events. He began to tap at his keyboard. "You know the rose she is wearing, pinned to her left shoulder?"

"Yes," I said wearily. You could hardly miss it. It was the most conspicuous single ornament to her attire, a large red flower symbolic of the red rose of the House of Lancaster. Although slightly crude and stylized compared with the inflorescences in the backdrop, it stood out like a pennant.

"Look at it carefully," he said. He then flashed it up, filling his screen with red petals and green under-leaves.

"Does anything strike you as strange?"

I scrutinized the screen. The rose looked like a rose, but then it dawned on me that there was a botanical anomaly. Instead of toothed leaflets (correctly indicated for roses in the painting's backdrop) it had large, lobe-shaped leaves, arranged in a rosette. There could be no mistaking what they were: the leaves of an English oak. Although it cannot be entirely ruled out that the artist was intending to imply that the Queen had the attributes of an English oak, an expression perhaps of fortitude in love when combined with a rose, there was no precedent for the oak as a symbol for Elizabeth: it would be a hundred years before the oak was informally recognized as a royal badge following the Restoration of Charles II, who during the Civil War had hidden, it is said, in an oak tree. There was one man, however, for whom the oak was a personal badge: Robert Dudley. This has been proved by a carved panel in the Tower of London, where he and his family had been briefly imprisoned, identifying members of the family by a symbolic botanical witticism playing on each name. Robert was labeled the Oak, a play on the tree's Latin name, *Quercus robur.*

An enthralling inference could now be drawn that the oak

leaves had been included, despite the formal message Elizabeth was sending to the nation at large, as a secret message to her lover. Bendor had been quietly progressing the theory over the past few days and was ready for my next question. Yes, he replied, Robert Dudley had indeed owned full-length portraits of Elizabeth—the two "greate [full-length] tables [panel paintings] of the quenes maiesties pictures" cited in the 1578 inventory of his pictures at Kenilworth Castle in Warwickshire. An art historian a few years earlier had attempted to match the identities of these two portraits with two other known paintings, but the argument was inconclusive and Bendor felt that the picture at Sotheby's could still be one of them. It was more than possible that the picture had initially belonged to Elizabeth, but, given her later desires to show herself in portraiture as a desexed virgin queen, it would have been given away as being awkwardly off-message for the palace walls, laced as it was with outdated marital and fertile allusions. Although family legend suggested that it was given by Elizabeth to Griffin Hampden, a very minor figure, there was no documentary evidence for this, and experience has shown such hand-me-down stories to be more often than not unreliable. The family could have acquired it much later, at any time following the dispersal of Dudley's collection after his death in 1588.

"Have you contacted Starkey yet?" I asked.

Bendor raised his eyebrows. I was underestimating his initiative.

"I e-mailed an image and details this morning—as well as my first thoughts about the constitutional crisis."

Thank goodness Bendor works for *me*, I reflected.

I left him to ruminate and dig while I considered other issues, namely the condition and the price. The following day I received a written report from Katherine Ara. She had minutely analyzed selected areas of the picture's surface and her inquisition ended with the conclusion I wanted to hear: "The restoration covering [the] areas of loss is unnecessarily extensive, crudely applied, and in places confused. The extent of wear to the areas of shell gold is more difficult to establish owing to the extent of the repainting. However when viewed in raking light the underlying ground appears to be largely intact. . . . " She had done as much as could be expected in the circumstances, and her conjectures concurred with my most optimistic hopes: we were closing in on a painting that, should we acquire it, and should it fulfill our expectations, could turn into a career event.

By the afternoon before the sale I was confident that we had enough insight to risk a very substantial amount of money. How much was still the question. It was unlikely that we would learn more before the following morning's sale at ten-thirty, and it was also time to make a recommendation to Alfred Bader, who was on Milwaukee time and would be asleep during the sale. I had no option but to run with what I had. In response to Bendor's e-mail Starkey had not produced anything of significance except that the picture greatly intrigued him, and a request for more time. He fully understood the relevance of seeking insight from the then current state of affairs, in particular the deputation of the House of Commons in January 1563 asking Elizabeth to name an heir—but her response to it was unrecorded. Speculation therefore remained, and in this respect the picture was no different from thousands of auction prospects I had considered before. The big difference was the stakes, which were giddily high.

Although every painting is unique, I tried to remind myself that this one had the potential to be *more unique* than others. In perfect condition and with full provenance and documentation—which we did not have—it would be an artifact of crucial historical stature, a work of art of transcendent significance and value to a range of sophisticated collectors and museums. With what we had been able to establish about its condition it was already likely to be worth more than three million, but I did not fancy having to wrestle a bid out of Alfred Bader at that level without more solid information. Although the final figure I was able to secure from Alfred has to remain commercially confidential, assistance of sorts came in the form of a phone call at around 5:30 P.M. that evening, and from the most unexpected quarter.

Journalists are key to our business. Among many other functions they flag big sales, report on them, reveal the names of buyers and sellers and promote the wares of auction houses and dealers. One particularly keen reporter had decided that Elizabeth was a picture to follow and so was calling to squeeze me for any indication that I might wish to buy it. Sensing that he might have more to divulge than I was prepared to give, I reversed the process and instead tried to squeeze him. Treating it as an opportunity to barter, he responded by telling me that he had just spoken to a prospective buyer who had claimed that he was going to buy it and, what was more, was preparing to bid £2 million. So certain was this unknown prospective buyer that he would buy it that with impulsive confidence he had spilled his heart to—of all people—a journalist. I traded back some anodyne thoughts about the uncertainty of the condition, and the pool of likely buyers, ending by telling him—truthfully—that I had made no clear bidding decisions.

I now had something directly to report to Alfred; and, in a sense, the auction had begun.

In comparison with auctions of modern pictures and old masters, those offering British pictures generate less heat, and that day the auction room was only half full. I had seated myself in an empty row four from the front, an optimum position to view lots as they mount the easel and retain uncluttered distance from the standing throng at the rear. Bendor, on the other hand, placed himself among the throng, where he could observe a different part of the action. A good deal taller than most of the ten or so dealers around him, from where he was standing he could both pick up on trade talk and enjoy a commanding view of the arena. With three lots to go I noticed that a number of telephone bidders were already chatting to prospective buyers. To avoid mishaps they normally contact their clients a few minutes in advance, and their timing was instructive. It was also more than likely that one of those standing at the rear next to Bendor would be secretly bidding via a member of their staff while looking on with apparent indifference—a seasoned ruse to throw the competition.

The auctioneer, Mark Poltimore, a colleague of mine on *Antiques Roadshow*, had been skipping through the lesser lots. A consummate professional, Poltimore has honed his rostrum skills with thirty years' experience in the art world. First at Christie's, followed by a spell as a dealer, and now as chairman of Sotheby's Europe, he combines puckish charm with all the auctioneer's dexterities, playing and reading the room with a conductor's confidence. Ominously he slackened his pace to announce the Elizabeth, catching my eye as he did so. When he opened at £500,000 a lady in the front row turned to smile at me. She looked familiar. Looking carefully at her companion I realized it was the radiologist, a bidding paddle in his hand.

There is an optimum time to enter the bidding, and it requires judging the hidden or anticipated actions of others. I duly waited. Poltimore gradually raised the increments, his smooth body language and glances keeping the room guessing. At £700,000 one of the telephones flagged him and he snatched the bid. Now that we had hit the lower estimate I knew we definitely had real bidders, and that the sale was live. I saw the radiologist speaking to his wife, but before he could lift his paddle—if indeed that was his intention—a bid came whistling over my head. I resisted the urge to turn and instead watched Poltimore bounce between the phone and the new bidder, rhythmically lifting the price. At £1.2 million it faltered.

The telephone bidder was spent, and I could also see the radiologist, who had yet to commit, locked in conversation with his wife. I waited until Poltimore fished his gaze across the room a second time and then met it with a nod. I had entered the game. Swiftly he swung back to the rear of the room, hooked another bid and then returned to me for more. I remained locked on Poltimore's face, meeting each return with a further bid. From where I was sitting I could hear the phones urgently relaying the escalating price, but the speed with which our increments were moving, at £50,000 a pop, left no space for interlopers, in less than a minute we had reached £2.1 million, and I was being asked for more. OK, I thought, we have cleared the psychological hurdle of the Big Two and now we shall see. I threw a further nod at Poltimore, who shot back a glance above my head. This time the glance did not immediately return. The opposition appeared to be wavering.

The auctioneer switched to seductive mode, craning forward and lowering his voice to lure a further increment. The rest of the room were now no more than observers. Just as I was expecting him to start winding up, his expression brightened. He had secured another bid and returned to me with a sprightly smile. Without even a momentary hesitation I punched back with another £50,000, and its speed had the bone-cracking effect I intended. Poltimore lifted his head, and then, failing to induce more from my adversary, cast his eye around the assembly, over to the telephone bidders and then back again to the underbidder for signs of life. All challengers had been thwarted. After what felt like an indecent pause, he raised his hand in what seemed like slow motion, and then clunked down the gavel. With auction commission the painting sold to me for £2.6 million.

Bendor gave me a brief sketch of the back-of-room antics after the sale. I had been underbid by another dealer, and he had noticed that at a lower level there were others about to enter, but the momentum was such that they had failed to break into the contest. Alfred Bader, whom I had telephoned that afternoon, was pleased with my success but, as the backer, was characteristically occupied with the payment terms, the cost of the restoration, how long it would take and what I would do with it next. As I read on Reuters that afternoon, I had offered the highest price ever paid for a British royal portrait at auction. Alfred had reason to be mindful.

When the picture was delivered that same afternoon, ushered through the doors like some visiting head of state, we all reverted to type. Bendor, animated by success, and still immersed in the portrait's historical challenges, proclaimed it the meatiest thing he could have hoped for. Tony Gregg, our South African in-house craftsman, known for taking his own line, was fixated on the frame. Emma Henderson, the gallery manager, fretted about our escalating insurance bill but found herself unable to take her eyes off the Queen's dress and jewels; while our front-of-house gallery assistant, Tamsin Evernden, was carefully processing her aesthetic response, as well as pondering the logistics of having so big a thing photographed.

I could barely lift my gaze from the image, feeling both triumphant and impatient—impatient to know how great a transformation would take place with cleaning, and where our research could take us next. I found myself particularly dwelling on the complexity of the fruit and flowers, which, under the gallery lights, were illuminated more strenuously than ever. Intriguingly, I noticed for the first time that each of these natural symbols was paired—each rose, fruit and bursting pea pod had its partner somewhere within the thicket.

The next morning, a Saturday, I woke exhausted from the week's adrenaline rushes. I normally escape to the Oxfordshire countryside each weekend, but I was grounded in London by other engagements. I decided to take the dog for a walk and gain some space and air, and having picked up a cup of Starbucks coffee I led our working black cocker spaniel into Kensington Palace Gardens. Laid out in the classical style by George II, the park has as its focal point a round lake, which that morning was bristling with bird life. Flotillas of ducks and geese vied with toy boats and competed for bread; from some distance I watched a pair of swans plunge from the sky into the water, their bodies enveloped in a great spray from which they glided off with unflustered grace. Nature, even urban nature, can be a therapy from the weekly dramas of the West End, and I felt badly in need of it that morning. I had just bought the most expensive picture of my life, it had been paid for by a man I wanted to do well for and there were still unanswered questions.

If I am honest, what first got me interested in art (and I had first done it with silver teaspoons and shoe buckles as a child) was the thrill of seizing on things others might have missed or undervalued. As a result I got to love the paintings I later moved on to. I and my colleagues may occupy a world of the ultimate luxury goods, of cosmopolitan refinement and intellectual acumen, but beneath the varnished surface the competitive animal lurks. That same predatory urge had just secured me the portrait of Elizabeth. In the disjointed mood I found myself in that morning, my thoughts drifted to my dog. All her instincts and joy, especially when she is in companionship with me, are to do with the chase. But, with the exception of the odd half-tame squirrel or unguarded picnic, there was no quarry for her that day, and she was reduced to following me at a slow trot. In the park there was no deep grass or undergrowth, no stream or copse, no opportunity to follow a scent with tail-wagging fury, as she does to exhaustion each weekend in the country. I have rarely known her to catch a pheasant, but the quest defines her existence, occupying her dog imagination, and I suspect providing her with those twitching, snuffling, squeaking dreams from which she occasionally wakes.

I too was now reduced to an unanimated trot in the cycle of this acquisition, anticipating a process that had every likelihood of being irksomely slow. The restoration of so complex a picture would take three or four months, and the historical research and its outcomes—well, they were anybody's guess. The hunting-instinct part was over and the picture now needed the specialist attention and consideration of others, which I could oversee but no longer control. As much as anything else, I suppose, I was suffering from a sense of anticlimax.

An Alsatian came bounding toward us and my spaniel froze in apprehension. The other dog then growled, and fearing a fight might ensue I bent down, attached the lead and marched her to the path for safety. As I did so my BlackBerry fell out of the loose top pocket of my tweed jacket, and retrieving and glancing at it I noticed I had a new e-mail. It was from David Starkey, to both me and Bendor. When we were working on the exhibition I had noticed that weekends were often his most productive times, as it was then, in the sanctuary of his library in Kent, that he could work with less distraction. I scrolled it down, wondering at first whether he was just asking whether we had bought the picture, but needless to say Bendor had told him. I quickly realized it was something of consequence and made for a park bench. Given that I value whatever Starkey has to say on historical matters, I have not deleted it:

Sorry not to have been able to get in on Thursday but ran out of time.

However, I think I've got the story. You were right about 1563. But we got the wrong bit. For there were TWO speeches on TWO separate occasions. We were thinking of the first, when a delegation of the Commons was received at Whitehall on 28 January. But it is the second that fits, when the Queen replied to the Lords on 10 April. She was present, though as customary in the Lords, the speech was delivered by Lord Keeper [Francis]

Bacon. But Elizabeth had written it. Indeed her holograph survives. And what a Manuscript!

"I had thought it had been so desired as none other tree's blossoms *should have been minded or ever hoped ere* my fruit *had been denied you . . .*

"But to the last, think not that you had needed this desire if I had seen a time so fit and it so ripe to be denounced . . . "

(BL, Lansdowne MS 94, art 15B, f. 30.)

I'd see the painting as the commemoration of this occasion. It makes sense of the chair and cloth of estate (the dominant feature of the Lords) . . . and the fruit and popping peas. And the Queen rather oddly standing between the two.

Best regards,

David

It was not till Monday that I got to discuss the e-mail with Bendor. He had with him a photograph of the original manuscript, which also showed the Queen's mind changes and crossings out, and we stood again before the picture as the early-morning light from the gallery's front windows lifted its presence, amplifying the thrilling recent advance. Bendor had already discussed the speech with Starkey and had concluded that its purpose was unambiguous. She was roundly responding to the 1563 Lords petition, employing characteristically embroidered rhetoric to do so. The underlying message was plain, even if the wording was not: she had no need to name a successor; she was well able to produce one of her own. Given the date of the portrait's execution, quite likely later that very year, this written evidence added a compelling dimension to the symbolic message.

One by one the visual sentiments proclaimed themselves like unfolding riddles. An affronted Queen, recently on her death-bed, was telling their Lordships, in as sovereign a way as possible, not to panic—that she could sort it out. This single assertion clarified everything: the suggestively ripe background became a riposte to the rumors that she was barren; the pairings within the vegetation a beckoning toward marriage—the only way a legitimate heir could be provided; her dress of red and white, the colors of the Tudor dynasty, a confirmation of readiness to continue the dynastic line, further affirmed by the throne and cloth of state; the gillyflower in her hand not in this case a symbol of betrothal but of a general willingness to commit.

It *could* have been interpreted as a marriage portrait with specific grooms in mind, but this construction barely touched on its underlying political urgency and topicality. This was an aging (by Renaissance standards) woman's clamorous assertion of self-determination—and with the benefit of historical hindsight its implicit promises were poignantly off target. The pomegranates, apples, pears, bursting pods and blossoming flowers were a pledge of progeny never delivered—a statement that would have increasingly undermined its subject in her succeeding years of spinsterhood. If it had belonged to her, as I had suspected all along, this alone would have been good enough reason quietly to dispose of it—and if so, why not to a past paramour for whom it would have been particularly emotive?

It was not just the painting's purpose but also the artist's identity that then evolved with research. The emergence of such important works of art often prompts researchers and new owners to revisit the primary documents that have given rise to art-historical assumptions. With rejuvenated resolve now that we had bought it, we made inquiries at the National Archives in Kew, a remarkable resource offering one thousand years of history from the Domesday Book to the present day. Over the next two months Bendor sifted through the relevant papers and wills to ascertain more about Steven van der Meulen, the Flemish artist to whom Sotheby's had attributed the painting. His research revealed an illuminating insight into a dark period of art history that still teems with mysteries, confusions and unsolved puzzles, that there was in fact no portraitist named Steven van der Meulen working for the court in London at the time, and that art historians had for the past century confused the identity of two Flemish artists who shared the same first name. The correct identity is now far more likely to be Steven van Herwijck—another Steven who was often referred to in sixteenth-century documents simply as "Steph. pictor," meaning "Steven, painter"—and not the comparatively obscure Steven van der Meulen.

The picture took five months to clean and restore, but the transformation was remarkable. It turned out that the surface was much better preserved than earlier feared, and although 40 percent of the image had been covered with overpaint, three-quarters of it was unnecessary and covering original paint. The gold began to shine, the dress and jewels returned to their former brilliance, the clouding film of leaching glue lifted. The Queen regained her background with convincing attachment. In the process of cleaning the possible Dudley connection became more conspiratorial. Paint analysis on the oak leaves surrounding the rose showed that while it was contemporary with the picture it was a different type of green from the foliage in the background: the oak leaves were of azurite (ground glass) mixed with lead-tin yellow; the foliage leaves in the background of copper glaze with an upper level of lead-tin yellow and greenish blue. The intriguing likely conclusion was that a different artist, using different compounds, had added it, but, to judge by its degradation and technique, clearly not long after the painting had been completed. Whether this was at the command of the painting's subject, or its recipient, or indeed someone else, may one day emerge.

My newly liberated Queen has since been acquired by a financier and art collector who assured me it will hang in the hallway of his country house. However, at the time of writing, in spring 2009, he allowed it to go on exhibition at Hampton Court Palace, the first port of call in what I suspect will be a century of new royal processions for the benefit of her public.

CHAPTER 6

A Winslow Homer Lost and Found

Almost every art discovery is a voyage of sorts, requiring the gathering of evidence, comparison and fact. Little did I know that May morning, as I blearily sank a fried breakfast at a hotel and repacked my overnight bag, that what would be tipped on my table an hour later would trigger a voyage in every sense, an odyssey that would take me from a stately home in England, via a dump in Ireland, to the beaches of the Bahamas.

For those who have only watched *Antiques Roadshow*— and there is now an audience that can claim to have done so for thirty years in England—the event needs to be visited in person to be fully understood. It is the BBC at its most lithe, fielding up to three thousand antique-bearing hopefuls toward a raft of experts at perpetually challenging historic locations. The American version of the show, an offshoot of ours, works along similar lines, and its veteran appraisers relate similar war-weary tales from the front line.

These onslaughts can be as punishing for the experts as for the production staff, who have to develop skills of tact and calm to deal with the expectations of the public. The queues can appear like immortal serpents, never ending and forever growing, each component part bearing an object, a story and the anticipation of a priceless discovery. By evening we often end up feeling siphoned of energy, and in dire need of a drink.

As locations go, the one up the road from my hotel that morning ranked high. The venue was Althorp, Princess Diana's childhood home in Northamptonshire, and among those milling in the crowd as I settled at my table was the young Earl Spencer, his puppy-dog features and shy smile poignantly reminiscent of his late sister. Although experience dictated that there is no correlation between the romance of the location and the quality of the day's objects, I felt expectant as I took my seat next to my pile of reference books and bottles of water—a fisherman's optimism that doggedly drives me, and many of my colleagues, through the day's challenges.

Although they were first in the queue, I did not fix my attention on the couple immediately, just the objects they produced, one by one, from plastic bags. Laid out before me in the early morning sunlight, they had the instant appeal of fresh goods. What do I mean by that? How can old objects look fresh? Very easily is the answer, particularly if you speed-date art and antiques for a living. In *Roadshow* terms, fresh means something of quality, un-tarted up, preferably scruffy, normally inherited, with a story to tell that triggers a thirst to know more. The owner's opening line was one I had heard many times before: "They are probably nothing," he said, "but I thought I would bring them along."

I looked up from the jumble of six pictures toward the voice. He was in his sixties, tall, white-haired, wiry, fit looking. Next to him was a woman in her midthirties, considerably shorter, with pronounced bangs that accentuated a round and pretty face. His accent was Midlands—I guessed he was local—and he shifted his weight back and forth as he spoke.

I immediately recognized the oil painting as a nineteenth-century copy of a Raphael, worth perhaps $300, but held back my response. Two months earlier I had told an old lady that her early-twentieth-century portrait of a young girl would be worth more if the child were better looking. She then revealed it was a portrait of herself as a child. From that moment I swore always to ask clients what they knew before wading in.

"So what can you tell me about them?" I asked.

He did not give an expected reply.

"I picked them up when I was out fishing in Ireland. I found them at my feet." He gesticulated downward to the lawn with his eyes. "Just lying there, in front of me."

Being a fisherman myself I tried to imagine how I might chance upon this disparate group of items around my wading boots. It was not easy to come up with a plausible scenario. Things like this had not happened on my fishing trips, but then again much stranger things had happened to dealers and collectors I know. I moved my gaze across the table, processing his oddball catch. Next to the Raphael copy was a print, probably early nineteenth century, a family group portrait by George Romney, the celebrated eighteenth-century portrait painter— of little value, but a rather cultivated subject, particularly when considered in the context of three of the other items: an unframed late nineteenth-century watercolor of a beach in the Bahamas inscribed as by Her Excellency Mrs. Blake (not a name that meant anything to me, but clearly something painted on location); next to it, insipid but well drawn, a continental sketch of a boy with a hawk that was clearly not British; and a framed invitation or flyer announcing an event called the Jamaica Exhibition, dated 1891, incorporating images of a worthy but unidentifiable late-Victorian couple.

My eye was primarily taken by a splashy and colorful watercolor of three children sitting beneath some palms. They were wearing exotic dress, Middle Eastern at a glance, and holding what appeared to be a chest of treasure with the startling form of a peacock fan at their feet. In the bottom right-hand corner was a penned signature, partially indecipherable. I picked up the watercolor and angled it into the sunlight. The first word was clearly readable: *Winslow*. Given that there are a finite number of well-known artists with that first name I was thus easily guided through the murkier form of the second name: *Homer*. I instantly checked myself. Surely not, I thought. I looked again at the figures, this time with a skeptic's eye. If this signature were real, I was looking at a work by one of the greatest painters in early American art history, a colossus of watercolor painting fought over by collectors.

The Homer legend began when *Harper's Monthly Magazine* sent him to the front lines of the American Civil War in 1861, from which he developed a series of war-related oil paintings that gained him his first critical acclaim. He moved to Prout's Neck on the Maine coast in his fifties and from there produced monumental seascapes and heroic dramas involving man's engagement with nature. The realism and power of these works established him as one of the most original and influential of

American painters. In later life, bolstered by financial security, Homer traveled to Florida, Cuba and the Bahamas, recording these trips with sparkling watercolors and sketches. I had never had the privilege of handling a Winslow Homer myself, but I had seen enough of the artist's work to know that three children in exotic dress sitting beneath what looked like an indoor potted plant was far from typical of his work.

"Could I possibly discuss this with my colleague?" I asked the man (his name turned out to be Tony), suppressing as well as I could any sense of anticipation. He happily agreed. Although already engaged with another visitor at our table, I managed to lure my co–picture expert, Clive Stewart-Lockheart, to behind a nearby garden statue where we could be alone, and I passed him the watercolor.

"Correct me if I am wrong, but I think this is Winslow Homer," I whispered. By this time I had managed a few more moments of reflection on the qualities of the picture, and had begun to notice crispness and certainty in the pencil work and the washes, particularly in the faces. With the combination of the convincing signature, I now had little doubt that something very exciting had landed on my table. Clive, a seasoned auction-eer and antiques generalist, as well as a particular expert on watercolors and oil paintings, scrutinized the signature with his magnifying lens, and then eyed the composition at arm's length.

"I think you are probably right," he said after a protracted silence, before adding, "Where the hell did he get it?"

"A fishing trip," I said.

He looked at me with total incredulity.

It was vintage *Roadshow*. Amid a crowd of onlookers, cameras and crew I was able to play Tony like a large bass, getting him to reveal the details of his fishing expedition, which, he explained, had taken place twenty years earlier in Youghal, County Cork, in Southern Ireland. He had found the pictures on the edge of a garbage dump that bordered the sea where he was fishing. They had remained in his attic ever since. I talked through the lesser pictures one by one, giving them small valuations, speculating on the worldly nature of the possible original owner, given their international range. Then I alighted on the watercolor. I showed him how I had deciphered the signature and explained Homer's significance as an artist who had himself traveled to Cuba and the Bahamas, and then I asked him if he could remember what he had caught that day.

"Just a spent flounder," he said.

"Well," I said, with theatrical timing, "you also netted a watercolor worth thirty thousand pounds." I went on to explain that it could be worth three or four times that if it were in better condition—diagnosing what I thought was fading, which I was later to revise.

The effect was palpable. Tony threw up his head and, in full view of the cameras, left the table on which the painting was lying to hunt out his daughter, Selina, the woman who had been with him earlier. I watched in silence as they embraced before he lumbered back to the table in mild shock to continue, falteringly, to express his delight.

Rustic Ireland can be both sublime and disappointing, and the promontory at Youghal was no exception. A glorious bay, studded with prominent houses and the Lego-shaped forms of white bungalows, was marred by the recycling center being constructed all around us. Tony was pointing to the raw stony ground beneath us, his fishing rod standing against the wire mesh of the dump fence. Summer had passed, as had winter, and very early spring flowers were beginning to push up along the steep banks of the path we had just walked. Standing next to me, with a television camera upon us, was Fiona Bruce, the iconic face of BBC television news, dressed in a red bomber jacket in startling contrast to the more formal outfits in which she apprises the nation of the world's events.

Things had moved apace since that scorching day at Althorp. Tony had given the watercolor to Selina, who had decided to enter it into an auction at Sotheby's, and the BBC, with an appetite sharpened by *Roadshow*'s success, had decided to commission a series of television programs on the subject of sleuthing art, to be jointly presented by Fiona and me. One was to be devoted to the Winslow Homer, which meant that the outcome of this random find by a fisherman had evolved from a private, life-impacting family event to a story soon to be shared with millions. It also meant that we had the means, and time, to aid its sale by adding the sort of information on the picture's history and provenance that art dealers rarely have the time or opportunity to do. Hence the dump.

As we drove from the ferry toward Youghal, Fiona and I had discussed how surprising it would be to find an unframed, unwrapped watercolor lying at your feet in Ireland, where it rains more often than not. Fiona, with her background in crime reporting, was particularly intrigued with this aspect of the find. The Homer could have been irreparably damaged in a downpour, and certainly the view of the Bahamas in gouache (thick watercolor pigment) would have been destroyed, so they can't have been there very long. And then there was the question of how they got there. Had they been abandoned by a naïve owner? Odd if they had. Or given away, and then thrown out as junk? Or had they, and this was an unsettling prospect, been stolen? In a sense this was not our problem: before an auction house agrees to sell a picture it has to satisfy itself on the subject of good title, or ownership, as best as it can. In any event, I saw it as my role to establish the history of the picture from the moment it was painted—its full artistic pedigree, rather than the complexities of rightful ownership. I am an art dealer, after all.

"This is where I found them, just lying here in a pile. The gate has now gone, but they were just outside," said Tony. He pointed to where a fence had once been. Beyond, the ground had a bulldozed flatness, suggesting that whatever dump had once been there had now been shifted or buried.

"Was anyone else around?" Fiona asked, slipping into her default investigative mode.

"No one I saw. I was alone fishing that day. But people used to come and go from here quite regular like. It's possible that they had just been dropped off a few hours earlier."

We were two miles from the town of Youghal, and although the town itself was out of sight, we were connected to it by a broad track and fairly busy road. Not that I felt the answer to this curious apparition would be found in your average town house. This was far from your usual yard sale discovery, something more rarefied. I thought again about each painting in the stack—where, or to whom, could they lead us? These were the chattels of sophisticated international travelers. They suggested owners who had crossed the boundaries of conventional existence, who were drawn to the exotic. Although from where we were standing we could not see the town, Youghal had once been a prominent port, a center of the textile industry, a place where things happened, though in recent centuries its fortunes had declined. I surveyed the distant landscape and noticed a number of prominent houses with their own grounds, some quite imposing. My guess was that somewhere on the horizon, or just beyond, lay our answer.

Bendor had not initially been as enthusiastic as I was about embarking upon this research project. I registered a lack of zest from the other side of his book-crowded desk when I first put it to him. It was hardly surprising. He had not been there at the moment of discovery, he had not carried out his normal style of methodical presale research, which he does do for all our stock-in-trade, and this was not a gallery purchase in which we were financially involved. I also had no images to show him that might trigger the inner bloodhound. It was only when the BBC accommodated us with a few stills from the film clip, which were surprisingly clear given that they were taken from television footage, that I noticed the stirrings of real interest.

To me these fly-tipped pictures were like the forensics at a major crime scene: tantalizingly suggestive but far from clear, and aching to be interpreted. I had already committed myself on national television to both a firm attribution to Winslow Homer and a chunky valuation, and was therefore keen to make sure that the picture had every chance of flying at sale. I could do without the need for embarrassing explanations or excuses if it failed. I had discovered that Selina had faced considerable hardship, single-handedly bringing up four children. This windfall would, among other things, allow her and her children for the first time to go on a group holiday abroad.

We hovered over the images on the screen and mulled over the clues and their implications, listing them one by one:

1. The Romney, the copy of the Raphael, and the continental drawing suggest travel and a level of education and sophistication.
2. The view of the Bahamas further suggests international exposure. It is inscribed as by Her Excellency Mrs. Blake. This is a firm name, and probably our most important lead.
3. The Winslow Homer is dated 1886. A quick Web search confirmed that he was traveling and painting in both Cuba and the Bahamas at this time.
4. The Jamaica Exhibition flyer is specifically dated to 1891 and has on it two photographic portraits of unknown individuals, a man and a woman. On closer inspection the man appears to be wearing a uniform of sorts.
5. All these objects were found in Youghal, Ireland.

The researcher in Bendor is stimulated by the achievable challenge. He likes to find the paw prints on the ground before he sets off on the chase. We agreed, come what may, that Bendor had first to crack the identity of Her Excellency Mrs. Blake, and the rest, with any luck, should follow. The term "Excellency" suggested diplomatic status, which could narrow the field considerably.

Art research involves the study of people as well as objects. In this sense it can feel like necromancy, digging up fragments of forgotten existences to which you can add an imaginative flourish and, hopefully, insight. So it was, as information began to pour in from various sources, that Bendor and I began to piece together the story of two epic lives that, had these pictures not surfaced, would most likely have remained forgotten to all but a few descendants.

The first person to emerge, by way of researching diplomatic records, was a man rather than a woman: Sir Henry Blake, governor to, in succession, the Bahamas, Newfoundland, Jamaica, Hong Kong and Ceylon. It quickly became clear that he had a remarkable wife too.

Their marriage had caused a scandal. Edith Osborne was the daughter of a wealthy political family from Clonmel in Ireland. An amateur artist and a naturalist, she was well traveled and highly educated, and young Henry, the son of a haberdasher who by then had become a county inspector in the Irish constabulary, was not the type of suitor her parents had had in mind. They eloped. Edith was disinherited, but Henry's career took off not too long after that. He was made one of five special magistrates invested with unprecedented powers during a lawless period of Irish unrest in the early 1880s. They led an imperiled existence, and Edith, who could count marksmanship among her accomplishments, protected her husband with a cocked pistol at her side when they traveled and attended court sessions.

Prestigious postings in the diplomatic service followed, and wherever the husband-and-wife team went they were recognized for progressive governance, as well as Edith's talent for classifying and recording nature with her delicate watercolors and her skill with languages. In Newfoundland, Blaketown is named after them, as is the flower on the Hong Kong flag, *Bauhinia blakeana*. Edith's record of the native moth population in Jamaica remains to this day an invaluable reference source in London's Natural History Museum. They also organized the National Jamaica Exhibition—the subject of the flyer in the group of pictures—and careful comparisons with other images of the couple in the National Portrait Gallery revealed that the unknown portraits on the flyer actually represented them at the time he was governor of Jamaica.

It is interesting how knowing the owner of a painting or antique can shape your visual response to it, in the same way that knowing the artist's life can. With the benefit of biographical insights gleaned from genealogical publications, diplomatic histories and the Internet, these dump finds now started to bristle with human significance. What had particularly interested me was the fact that in 1872 Edith had embarked upon a one-year trip to the Continent, visiting Greece, Malta, Sicily, Italy and Austria—a sort of Grand Tour to enrich the mind. With a little imagination I was now able to see the modest drawing of the shepherd, the copy of the Raphael and the Romney as possible keepsakes by someone in thrall to European culture; the view of the Bahamas became the thoughtful record of an intrepid woman painter, linguist and naturalist; and the flyer from Jamaica the poignant testament to a remarkable diplomatic career that had spanned the British Empire. The jewel in the crown, the Winslow Homer, clicked into place with similar neatness. In 1884 Homer was in the Bahamas to illustrate an article about Nassau, the port city of this tropical island.

Although he later embarked for Cuba, the date was highly significant. Eighteen eighty-four was the first year of Sir Henry's three-year governorship of the Bahamas, and, given the Blake's diplomatic functions and Edith's artistic leaning, it was more than likely that they would have met up with America's premier illustrator and watercolorist while he was out there.

Bendor likes to keep the best for last. He had been digging away into the final years of the Blakes, and unknown to me had discovered that in retirement they had returned to their native Ireland. Not just anywhere in Ireland, however.

"Does the name Myrtle Grove mean anything to you?" he asked.

"Why should it?" I replied.

He now assumed the cocky look of a barrister delivering the final paragraph of a winning argument.

"It's a Tudor house which by repute was once the home of Sir Walter Raleigh, for a start. It later became the retirement home of the Blakes, and sounds like a rather fascinating place. It's also about two miles away."

"From here?" I asked, imagining a now lost house somewhere on the outskirts of central London.

"No. From the dump!" he said. "It's in Youghal."

All manner of thoughts now flashed through my mind. Apart from the obvious ones about how these objects might have bodily moved from the Blakes' house to the dump, we had fingered an almost certain first-stage provenance, the diplomatic couple. Although the watercolor was not topographically clear, and the scene could be of Cuba, there was every chance it had been painted in the Blake's city of residence at the time, Nassau. This was the sort of circumstantial evidence that could significantly add to the watercolor's status and value. Was there, I now wondered, any evidence that Homer knew or came into contact with the Blakes in Nassau? Bendor could not answer that question.

"I have done as much as I can in London. You will need to go to the Bahamas to find out more."

I felt the beaches beckoning and wondered whether a television budget would stretch to cover a trip to the Bahamas.

Sotheby's, in New York, had been selected by Selina, and I prepared a brief description of our findings on provenance to help the cataloguers catch the deadline for a sale at the end of May. The auction house's approach was two pronged. The first was to establish that there were no records of a stolen picture or pictures that fit these descriptions, and they began steps to contact the family. Myrtle Grove still stood, and from what I could gather there were family descendants who continued to live there. The second was to show the Homer to Abigail Booth Gerdts, the art historian currently compiling a catalogue raisonné of the artist's work, in order to give the painting the certification of authenticity. This worried me slightly. Homer was a painter of the outback. He delighted in the rendition of rural life, of fishing trips and dramas, nature at its most animated, the crashing wave, the jumping fish, storm clouds, and bending trees. In this respect he had the instincts of an action photographer to which his sublime skills in paint could give form—fifty years before others did so with a camera. A group of ornately garbed children in an interior was hardly part of his stock-in-trade. It would most likely cause the auction house's chosen authority to scratch her head long and hard before committing.

One of the BBC's film directors was with Selina filming at her home in Coventry when a telephone call came through from Sotheby's. Selina was ecstatic to hear that the Homer had been given a clean bill of health: it was now deemed fully authentic. Not only that, but with the likely provenance and comparison with other known works from Homer's tropical jaunts, the estimate had now jumped to $150,000–$250,000. By the time the catalogue came out, three weeks before the sale, the auction house was satisfied following its inquiries that nothing now stood in the way of Selina's title of ownership. It had duly been published with a splashy, full-page illustration, together with a catalogue note and provenance details that speculated, rather than stating with certainty, that the picture had once been owned by the governor and his wife. Gerdts's view was that it was more likely to have been painted in Cuba than in the Bahamas.

Selina's family had galvanized themselves for the life-changing sale. She had put down a deposit for a family trip to Disney World, and she, her partner and Tony now decided to visit America for the first time to attend the sale and spend a week getting to know New York. For me the news was a huge relief. The painting now had the sort of imprimatur that would satisfy important collectors and dealers and, partly as a consequence, Sotheby's was fueled with commercial ambition. It was the best outcome I could have expected. This work on paper had come a long way since the morning it dropped on my table at Althorp.

There was still an element of unfinished business, and it lay in the West Indies. Carefully considering the budget, the program producer had found the funds to send a film crew to Nassau, which now opened up the possibility of adding yet more transformative knowledge to the picture's history. There was a chance, just a chance, that somewhere on the island of the Bahamas was information that could link Homer directly with the Blakes, and throw light on the watercolor's unusual subject matter, and we felt by now it would be irresponsible to leave this stone unturned. After careful discussions, and with a week to go before the sale, it was decided that I should go out there on my way to New York. Fiona would remain in Coventry with Selina's four children to film their reaction to the sale results when their mother phoned them through—a division of responsibilities that felt a little unequal as I was looking for my sunglasses and shorts the night before I left.

There was no guarantee that I would return from the Bahamas with anything useful. Earlier experiences of researching in tropical climes had taught me that documents, newspapers, bills of sale, deeds and so forth were not nearly as well preserved there as in more temperate places. The humid, insect-ridden climate in Jamaica, for example, had caused many historical documents to literally decompose.

I have to admit to a degree of disappointment as I left the airport and drove along the coast road to Nassau. I had carried with me an iconic image of silver sands, palm trees, azurite seas and the crumbling remains of colonial empire, but this romantic vision slowly dismantled itself as I passed yet another hotel, metal road sign, garage or advertising billboard, offering the initial impression of a damper, warmer suburbia. It was not assisted by a stiff wind, overcast skies and the awkward absence of any decent vista for the film crew to capture the romantic cliché. Things started to look up after I checked in at my hotel and, later that afternoon, began to explore the center of the old town by foot. The sun had also returned.

I mounted steep stone steps that led to an icing-pink neo-classical building capped with a prominent pediment. Long-shuttered windows, vents for the sea breezes, flanked the door, distinguishing its design from anything in Europe, as did the whitewashed statuary and exotic vegetation in the forecourt and surrounding gardens. This was Government House, the old seat of Her Majesty's Governor, and, feeling myself back in the time of the Blakes, I now began to connect with my quest. Two armed black soldiers in starched white uniforms stood nonchalantly before the front door, a reminder that this was still the working government residence it had been in the days when the young haberdasher's son and his wife arrived for their first posting overseas. We had gained permission to film inside the next morning, but for now this was just an exploratory jaunt, a means of preparing myself for the next episode in a breakneck day-and-a-half visit. The BBC wanted me back in New York for the sale, and my main target was the National Archives of the Bahamas, a nondescript building on the edge of the old town. I lingered as long as I could in the garden paradise and then set off.

I am not used to working with a cameraman, a director, a soundman and a researcher watching my every move. They positioned themselves at my side and over my shoulder and for a brief moment I felt a sympathy for the overphotographed gorillas. Above my head a green lizard artfully stalked a moth. The room was humid, and as the archivist loaded the microfilm I began to reflect on the extraordinary chain of events that had taken me from a table in the garden of one of England's great stately homes to a musty old colonial archive on the other side of the Atlantic. Although there was no guarantee that we would find anything of consequence, at least I was now excavating a place and time from which the watercolor may have come into being.

I did have two advantages. The only newspaper of consequence during the period was the *Nassau Guardian*, and its early editions were on microfilm, through which I could scroll on a rather ancient, creaking machine. I also had a date that allowed me to home in on the right months. It was an established fact that Winslow Homer arrived in Nassau from Maine in the first few days of December 1884 in the company of his father—their arrival had been officially recorded. He had been commissioned to paint here by the *Century Magazine*, which was responding to the increasing popularity of the Bahamas as a tourist resort. Travel guides for the island had begun to be published in both London and New York, praising it for its beauty and temperate climate, aspects that no doubt appealed to Homer and his father, who were not incidentally escaping the harsh New England winter.

Scrolling through the dense news sheets, it was clear that Nassau had been thrumming with commerce; interspersed with announcements of official business and the comings and goings of visitors were advertisements for boarding schools on the mainland of North America, new stores and retailers and detailed descriptions of the latest imports, including cure-all tonics for the infirm. It soon became clear in this clatter of life that the *Guardian* had an official function. Numerous paragraphs on the front and inside pages began with the words "His Excellency the Governor..." and normally referred to some government pronouncement or event. I focused on these, not just because they were references to Henry Blake, but because they often included the names of other islanders and visitors, among whom there was a chance that Winslow Homer could feature. This was old-style research that generations of historical investigators had been obliged to perfect. How much quicker, I reflected, it would be if these papers were online, and all I needed to do was to pop "Winslow Homer" into a search box. Instead I had to train my own eyes to act as search engines.

I spotted him after about half an hour among an unusually dense list of names. It made me jump, and I signaled the director to get the camera going. On January 3, 1885, the *Nassau Guardian* reported that the Blakes had held a children's fancy dress ball at Government House. Among those attending was a "Mr. Homer." This was an electrifying advance. From the corner of my eye I could see the cameraman pulling in for a close-up as I began to narrate aloud what I had found. I had encountered the first positive link between Homer and the Blakes. There was much more in the next column. Clearly it must have been a slow news day, as exhaustive detail was expended in describing the childrens' costumes, and none more so—to my growing excitement—than those of the governor's children, who were dressed as "Arabian Knights."

They were listed one above the other:

Miss Blake: Princess Perizide

Master A. Blake: Prince Bahman

Master M. Blake: Prince Perriz

The anonymous reporter was clearly enraptured by the event, and by the governor's family in particular: "In their richly embroidered dresses and with their fair faces, [they] would have made a most picturesque group which we would like to see retained in some substantial form."

This was more than I could ever have expected: a description of the three young Blake children (who I had not until then known existed) that corresponded almost exactly to the watercolor! The reporter, with prophetic insight, had suggested that in their party clothes they should have been recorded for posterity—i.e., painted or photographed. And one of the greatest American artists of his time was reported as being present at the party. If this had been a crime scene, the evidence could not have been more complete. I had always assumed that the Homer was a general subject picture painting (that is, a rustic subject, rather than formal portraiture) but now it all seemed so obvious. Although Homer was not a portrait painter, in the Bahamas that New Year he was the next best thing. Edith, an artist herself, would have been quick to make his acquaintance and—with what combination of flattery and insinuation we will never know—this great artist of nature and the frontiers was persuaded to redirect his brush toward her three costumed children.

With two days to go before the sale, although late in the day, Sotheby's was delighted to receive the news of this further discovery. A written salesroom notice was quickly affixed next to the watercolor, which had now been cleaned, framed and mounted. It seemed to glow with self-esteem on the viewing-room wall, now that it was in the company of other great American masters. Tony and Selina had attended a viewing party the night before, and told me how much they were enjoying their time in New York. Wherever they went they were attended by a BBC cameraman, and Selina had emerged with star quality, communicating her first responses to the Big Apple, and the intimidating process of the international art world, with beguiling clarity and freshness.

She was little prepared, however, for the telephone call she would receive that afternoon before the sale. Shortly before she said good night to her youngest children in England, Sotheby's telephoned her with news she could barely fathom. Someone, an unknown party, had claimed that the picture was theirs. She had been given the option of withdrawing it from sale or letting it sell and settling for 25 percent of the proceeds. Sotheby's was obliged to respond to the claim, as they always are in these circumstances, by doing nothing until it had been settled.

We met up the following day at Sotheby's. Selina looked agitated, but she had resolved to see the sale through and deal with the fallout afterward. As the auction room chairs began to fill with prospective buyers, she hung around the back of the room with the BBC crew and her father. Her voice sounded strained, but the same indomitable spirit that had carried her through her own intrepid voyage was in evidence now. She told me of the "roller coaster" of emotions that had begun the day of my attribution at Althorp, the impact that it had had on her family, yanked from their familiar routine by this life-changing event, and how this unforeseen challenge seemed part of a pattern of unpredictability she had been up against all her life. More than anything else, she sounded angry that it had taken till now, after all the research and investment and time, for someone to make a claim on her father's catch. She was adamant that whoever, or whatever, had come out of the unknown would not now unseat her; she would see this through with the same drive and instinct she had applied to everything in her life so far.

The Homer was lot 16, and I took a seat at the back of the room as the auctioneer called the room to order. I had managed to have a brief chat with a couple of American dealers I knew, one of whom—well plugged in to the likely buyers—thought that the picture would almost certainly sell within estimate, particularly with its recent added provenance. This was quite a relief. Failure to sell is a constant fear for all those who place pictures in auction: however extensive and bullish the marketing and expectations of the auction house, particularly during the recent recession, up to 40 percent of the paintings in some sales have had to be returned unsold, or contritely reoffered in a later sale, at a lower price. This was May 2009: the papers were full of stories of disappointing auction results and unsold masterpieces.

I began annotating my catalogue as the first pictures began to fall beneath the gavel. The mood of the auction—something that can become quickly detectable to both the buyers and auctioneers—felt as yet undecided. A few of the prices looked encouraging, but the odd failure checked any optimism. With ten lots to go I turned around to notice Selina, with uneasy body language, talking to someone beyond the entrance to the auction room. This surprised me. She was meant to be upstairs in a viewing room with a sound system and lofty view of the auction proceedings (a privilege offered to special vendors who wish to remain separate from the action). I then received a whispered request in my ear from our researcher Laura to join the crew, who were no longer filming the auction.

As I approached the back, a group of unrecognizable faces from legal and the press marched from the elevators. Selina, pale and shocked, now found herself being addressed by not one person, but a phalanx of officials. I stood beside her—joined by a television camera and a boom microphone. She listened blankly as an in-house Sotheby's lawyer clarified the situation with bespectacled impassivity: the unknown claimant had changed his position, and had requested that the picture be withdrawn from sale unless she accepted an offer, now upped to 30 percent of the proceeds. In such situations—and I partly knew this from my own experience—the auction house has no choice but to wait until both parties have come to terms. In the event that they fail to reach an agreement, the auction house will hold onto the picture until proper title can be proved, and then take instructions from the legal vendor. They were sensitive in their wording but adamant in their resolve. Selina was equally clear: there was no way she would accept the deal. With barely three lots to go, instructions were relayed to pull the Winslow Homer from the sale. A Sotheby's legal spokesman later told me that in fifteen years he had never known this to happen so close to the wire.

Nicola Lafferty, the BBC's director, discreetly identified a man in his thirties standing on the edge of our gathering. Of smallish build, with thick black hair and a distinctly British appearance, he was the unknown claimant, she told me. What was more, she added, he had indicated that he was happy to talk, and we were offered a room at Sotheby's where this conversation could take place. It was as if we had rubbed a lamp and released a genie: here was a direct descendant of the children whose portrait had come into my life with no history or context or meaning. Simon Murray, as he later introduced himself, was the great-great-grandson of Henry and Edith Blake, and despite Sotheby's attempts to contact any likely claimants, which they affirmed were considered and methodical, it was only their press release a week before the sale, which had included an image of the picture and its possible provenance, that had summoned him from the ether. Or London, to be more precise.

As a specialist in historical portraiture, I always find it intriguing to match a descendant's face to a portrait. But it was not the blurry photographs of Henry and Edith Blake that came to mind as Simon Murray sat before me in the windowless room we had been given for our interview. It was their biographies: the globe-trotting diplomat and his risk-taking naturalist wife. Simon Murray was a career barrister; he had turned from criminal to civil practice, and in a reasoned and thoughtful manner he stated his claim. His sister lived at Myrtle Grove. There were no crime reports of these pictures' having been stolen from the house twenty years ago as far as he knew, and he did not know how they got from the house to the dump. He had also never heard of Winslow Homer. That the paintings were once in his family's possession, however, he had no doubt, and that was sufficient for him to hold up the sale and make the claim. He also added that Myrtle Grove was in a dire state of disrepair and the funds from the sale of this picture could usefully assist.

I said goodbye to Selina and Tony that afternoon before leaving for the airport. Tony had a hangdog expression and seemed resigned, but a robust confidence had begun to surface in Selina, who waylaid me before I left.

"We have got this far, and spent all this money we did not have, and I am not going to be bullied into giving up what I feel is rightly ours," she said. "They may think they can, but they do not know me well enough. We shall fight it in every way we can."

As this book goes to press in February 2010, a negotiated resolution has yet to be reached. Two families continue vehemently to lay claim to a major piece of art whose value, significance and even existence were, until very recently, largely unknown to them. That the watercolor and other pictures had once been in the ownership of the Murray family there is no doubt, and Simon Murray has since found family documents to further prove it. How they got to the dump and thus into the possession of Tony is an issue yet be resolved. Although no formal records of a theft have been produced, Murray is now claiming that they were stolen; he had earlier told me that youths from the town would occasionally break into the outhouses of Myrtle Grove, and that it is quite possible that these and other objects—their significance overlooked—were stored there, where their loss could have passed unnoticed.

Whatever the outcome of this unfortunate spat, anonymity is a fate that this painting is never likely to have to endure again.

Acknowledgments

There is a host of helpful and long-suffering friends and acquaintances without whose collaboration this would not have moved from a sketched thought, suggested to me at a dinner party, into this book.

The dinner in question was given by Bruce and Lucinda Palling, who sat me next to Vicky Barnsley, managing director of HarperCollins in London. Had their seating plan been different, or their wine less drinkable, the consequences would not have developed as they did. Three months later Elizabeth Sheinkman came into my life as my agent and, with charm, perseverance and a Manhattan drive from which we all have something to learn, struck a deal which allowed me to unmoor myself from the gallery, get on planes and adhere to a laptop for more hours than I can dare count—time I would otherwise have spent buying and selling pictures and living a family life. I came to rely on my gallery staff, including Bendor Grosvenor (a protagonist in three of these chapters), Emma Henderson and Sara Denham, who managed to get by unsettlingly well without me and who contributed to the book with words, ideas, responses and encouragement. I also owe thanks to those who regularly supply their expertise to our business and proved invaluable as sounding boards for this book—in particular Rebecca Gregg, who rose hearteningly to the challenge, and Katherine Ara.

Rachel Kaminsky has been invaluable. She gave me ideas, followed them up with leads and then acted as reader for the whole text. Although I take responsibility for any mistakes herein, I would like to acknowledge with profound gratitude her punctilious questioning and professional responses, both as a highly experienced dealer and ex-auctioneer and as someone with a wry understanding of human nature in the art world and beyond.

Early on in my research, waiting for planes in Jacksonville, Florida, that seemed incapable of touching down, I got into a long dialogue with a woman whose inspiration has remained with me. She gave me a number of approaches that I then carried through the book: whoever you are, wherever you are, I wish I could acknowledge you other than by the coy epithet of my "Jacksonville muse."

The kindness of those who have allowed themselves to be interviewed and autopsied, and who then went on to give yet more of their time and generosity in providing images and checking facts, has been profound. I would especially like to thank Toni Newton, who gave me more assistance than an author could dare hope or ask for. I count her as an ally in this project and am also indebted to the hospitality and kindness of her husband, Clark Townsend, and her perennially young mother, Jo. John Sunderman, Earle Newton's old friend and adviser, is also to be thanked, as is Barry Buxton of the Savannah College of Art and Design. Don Trachte has been a sterling supporter, and is another who has gone to unusual lengths to help me. In addition I would like to acknowledge the collaboration and help of Linda Perot, Professor Ernst van der Wetering, Oliver Barker, Frank Dunphy, and Alfred and Isabel Bader.

Bob Pullen put me right on the Astor family, and Lucy Fenwick, a mainstay of Sotheby's British Pictures department, on a number of facts and insights from the auction world. Thank goodness for friends who are prepared to give of their time and support.

Anyone who has written a book will know how important the backroom figures are in helping create the finished product. Joy de Menil of the Penguin Group (USA) has been an inspiring and constant support. She and her team have diligently edited the book, to ensure that my words reach the audience for which they are intended. Simon Shaw of *Antiques Roadshow* has been a supporter of this endeavor from the outset and one of the first reader guinea pigs. I would like to thank him too.

My father has been, as he always is, the perfect combination of pedagogue and pastor. Reading the drafts of my first two chapters, bolstering me with optimism and then offering himself as unpaid editor to rectify what he described as my literal errors was exactly what a father should do and I am indebted to him and my late mother for their encouragement and support throughout my career. Parents, particularly fathers, seem to surface rather often in this book and they need to be kept in mind as valuable potential resources for navigation, even for the middle-aged.

Index